W9-CCN-322

SOME TRADITIONAL AFRICAN BELIEFS.
◼ [a beginner's guide] ◼

KATE RHEEDERS

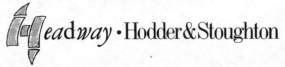 **Headway** · Hodder & Stoughton

1. CULTURE -- AFRICA
5. AFRICA -- CIVILIZATION
I. TITLE

Order queries: please contact Bookpoint Ltd, 39 Milton Park, Abingdon, Oxon OX14 4TD. Telephone: (44) 01235 400414, Fax: (44) 01235 400454. Lines are open from 9.00 - 6.00, Monday to Saturday, with a 24 hour message answering service. Email address: orders@bookpoint.co.uk

British Library Cataloguing in Publication Data
A catalogue record for this title is available from The British Library

ISBN 0 340 70471 3

First published 1998
Impression number 10 9 8 7 6 5 4 3 2 1
Year   2003 2002 2001 2000 1999 1998

Typeset by Transet Limited, Coventry, England.
Printed in Great Britain for Hodder & Stoughton Educational, a division of Hodder Headline plc, 338 Euston Road, London NW1 3BH by Cox and Wyman Limited, Reading, Berks.

This book is dedicated to my friend and tutor, Nomvula, who spent many long nights patiently teaching me the African way.

Special thanks to Eyal Sarig for helping me find the balance necessary to work with this knowledge.

Thank you to Michael Scallan for his patience and much appreciated feedback while proof reading my manuscript.

My final thank you goes to Femke Snyman who so lovingly put together the illustrations.

CONTENTS

Introduction   1

Chapter 1   Southern African History   4

Nguni tribe   6
Sotho tribe   9
Venda tribe   12
Tsonga tribe   12
Today's African   13

Chapter 2   Family Structure   16

Staple diets   16
Traditional dress   17
Settlements   19
Growing up   21
Puberty   23
Adult life and marriage   24
Death   26
Legal systems   27

Chapter 3   African Beliefs   29

The creator   29
Death   30
Ancestral spirits   31
Princess of Heaven   32
The Snakes   33
Masks and drums   33

Chapter 4   Witchcraft and sorcery   36

Witchcraft	37
Sorcery	38
Protection	39
Elimination	39
Pollution	40

Chapter 5   African divination   43

Health	43
The calling	44
The apprenticeship	44
The initiation	45
Divination	46
Diagnosis	47
Medicine	47

Chapter 6   Divination tools   50

Venda divination tablets	50
Casting the tablets	51
Other divination bones	52
Other necessary tools	57
The procedure	58

Chapter 7   Western similarities   60

Element tablets	60
Sangoma bones	64
Summary	71
Divination Mat	73

Chapter 8   Sample readings   77

Feedback   89

INTRODUCTION

For the purpose of this book, to avoid the distracting clutter of semantic discourse, I will refer simply to 'black' and 'white' Africans and at no time use these words in a racist manner. Furthermore, 'black' does not signify bad/evil and neither does 'white' signify good/pure. I have chosen to use these words in a sense to demystify the jargon of apartheid. It was, after all, a system of opposites; black versus white.

I was born into a large white South African family during the Apartheid era when blacks were oppressed by whites. A brief summary of the history behind these laws is given in Chapter 1. Although my ancestors were originally from Europe (Scotland and Germany), we spoke Afrikaans (a Dutch dialect) at home and we were a typical example of a family born on the 'right' side of the colour barrier in a racially segregated society.

During my early years my parents were rather poor and, unlike other white families, they did not employ black domestic servants. I therefore had no contact with black people and, as a result, I often found myself fantasising about their traditions. Like Yin-Yang, life then existed around black and white opposites, with very little, if any, grey in between. When something was understood by those around me it was accepted as part of the white side of life while whatever was foreign obviously belonged to the opposite pole of existence: the 'black' side.

I realise now that I must have been a difficult child to deal with as I always needed detailed explanations. At the age of five I had my first mystical encounter. Not only was it the start of my search for truth, but it also brought me face to face with the reality of life in Africa.

1

I had a habit of spinning on the spot until I lost my balance and fell down, while my head continued to spin. On one particular day it felt as if I continued to spin upwards until I finally reached the sun.

With childlike enthusiasm, I ran inside and told everyone that there was a ball of fire in the sky. This was obviously not understood and I was scolded for telling lies. Scowling I went back into the garden where I saw a vision of a mature lady dressed in a turquoise caftan. She told me that she believed me and that one day I would understand. This vision kept my search for truth alive for many years, but that is another story.

I realise now that I began associating my feelings, especially my mystical experiences, with the opposite pole of what I then perceived existence to be. Slowly I began disassociating myself from the white belief system and doubted everything I was taught. For a long time I truly believed that the only reason I was white was due to my daily scrub. I thought that, if I went without a bath for long enough, my family would discover that I did not belong with them and I would be returned to my black mother.

My sorry state continued for a number of years until one day, at the age of eight, a black woman entered my life for the first time. I felt at home. My sadness soon lifted and suddenly I became exposed to a different side of life. I learned with great eagerness from all the black people that entered my life from that day on. However, my greatest teacher came into my life during my twenties: my friend Nomvula.

Nomvula was born into a black African family of the Ndebele tribe. The dialect she spoke was very similar to Afrikaans so communication was easy. She was a traditional healer who, in later years, went on to study conventional medicine. This gave Nomvula a wonderful balance that she uses today to improve the lives of those who seek her advice.

This book contains many of the interesting facts about Southern African traditional beliefs and practices that I have learned from my friend and teacher Nomvula.

EXERCISE 1
SPINNING THE INNER CHILD

The spinning experience shared with you earlier, has played a major role in my life and continues to do so to this day. It has a strong grounding effect while simultaneously allowing the creative energies to flow. I feel that this exercise is an appropriate place to start our journey into African traditions.

Find yourself a clear patch of grass. Stand with your feet together, arms outstretched, and close your eyes. Starting with your right foot, slowly start turning clockwise, taking very small steps. Avoid taking big steps as this will widen the circle to the point where you may lose control. Spin yourself until you start feeling light-headed.

Allow yourself to fall gently on to your back and, while keeping your eyes shut, become aware of the spinning sensation coming from the pit of your stomach. Imagine your inner child being free from the limitations placed upon it and feel this child spinning while standing on your body. At the same time, become aware of your body sinking deeper and deeper into the soil until you are one with the earth.

As the dizziness fades, imagine the child slowly settling down and coming to rest on top of you. Open your eyes and look at the sky through the eyes of the child. Enjoy the wonder of the clouds and notice the vast emptiness displayed above you. Connect the hidden pictures in the clouds to experiences in your life by using the wisdom of your age and the innocent, uncluttered vision of your external inner child.

SOUTHERN
AFRICAN HISTORY

*A*ccording to archaeologists, black Africans have lived in the
*Transvaal area of Southern Africa since 350 AD and are, in terms
of population, by far the majority in modern Southern Africa. There are
many aspects of African life that remain unchanged, even though
various influences have had an effect on their society and beliefs.*

Ancient African history was passed from generation to generation in
the form of stories, while another common form of expression was
through art. Aspects of life were generally recorded in art and these
objects were then used in ceremonies and rituals. This will be
discussed further in Chapter 3.

Due to the lack of written material on the history of the tribal people
of Southern Africa, the period prior to the birth of Christ may therefore
be pure myth or legend. This knowledge was passed down orally for
many generations. Chapter 3 discusses some of these issues.

Southern African culture has been dated to almost 2,000 years ago
when tribes began to move south of the Limpopo River. It is believed
that they remained there for approximately 1,000 years, farming
crops and raising cattle. The latter was limited, probably, due to
malaria and tsetse fly and the people relied more and more on their
crops.

It is believed that there were four original tribes. Two large tribes –
the Nguni and Sotho and two smaller tribes – the Venda and
Tsongo. The Nguni tribe was divided into the Xhosa, Zulu, Swazi
and Ndebele groups while the Sotho group was divided into the
Tswana (also referred to as West Sothos) and the South and North

Sotho groups. It is presumed that before the migration took place a dialect of the same language was shared by these tribes.

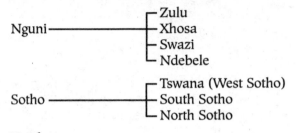

Nguni ——————
- Zulu
- Xhosa
- Swazi
- Ndebele

Sotho ——————
- Tswana (West Sotho)
- South Sotho
- North Sotho

Venda
Tsongo

Map of Southern Africa

NGUNI TRIBE

The first tribe to move south were the Nguni, breaking up into smaller groups with the majority settling in what is presently known as KwaZulu Natal. Due to the rich soil and ideal pastures in this area they became mainly cattle keepers, with milk and beef as their staple diet. The importance of cattle affected every aspect of their lives and this is clearly evident in their rituals and cultural beliefs. Their language gradually changed as they were influenced by other tribes they encountered. As they started spreading themselves over a large area they retained aspects of their Nguni culture in scattered settlements.

Zulu people

Due to their military successes under the leadership of Shaka between 1817 and 1828 the Zulu are probably the best known African people. Although similar to the Xhosa in custom and language, the systems of the Zulu people changed late in the eighteenth century with the emergence of large political groups. This reached its zenith under Shaka, son of Senzangakhona. By 1819 he was the undisputed leader of the people between the Pongola and Tugela rivers.

Shaka placed his men in regiments according to their age, which meant that fathers and sons were separated, and men from different districts were mixed, resulting in a decrease of rivalry between the smaller groups. Shaka also used his older female relations to keep an eye on younger men. The biggest reason for his success was in the training of his warriors. They fought barefoot, which increased their speed, and the throwing type of assegai or spear was replaced with a stabbing one. This encouraged hand-to-hand combat, in which they proved to be unbeatable.

Shaka, often referred to as the 'African Napoleon', used a battle tactic similar to Napoleon's. It is referred to as the bull-horn tactic. Shaka's warriors attacked in the shape of a horn, encircled the enemy and slowly closed on them, ensuring that no-one survived the fight.

A young Zulu warrior

No man was allowed to marry before the age of forty and only then would he be transferred to the reserve regiment for older men. Shaka channelled the sexual energy of his warriors into battle-ready aggression. Every regiment had one leader who was directly answerable to Shaka. He ruled with an iron fist and like most dictators made enemies. He was murdered by his own servant and two half-brothers, Dingane and Mhlangane, in 1828. Dingane later had his brother Mhlangane killed and took over the kingdom. His forces attacked the Voortrekkers, killing their leader, Piet Retief, but were eventually defeated at the battle of Blood River in 1838.

The Zulus never regained the status they enjoyed during Shaka's rule. Once the British invaded Natal they were weakened even more, the tribes being divided into thirteen smaller groups with individual chiefs appointed by the state. However, during the peak period of Shaka's rule the tribe had a profound influence on all those they encountered and this is evident in the changes that occurred in other tribes.

Xhosa people

Xhosa and Zulu are today the most widely spoken African languages in Southern Africa, with over 6 million Xhosa-speaking people. The Xhosa people seem to have been the first migrating tribe to come into contact with other indigenous peoples of Southern Africa. One such group was the 'Khoisan', a term referring to two groups conventionally divided: the Khoikhoi (Hottentots) who kept cattle and sheep and the San (Bushmen) hunter-gatherers. Some Xhosa tribes are of mixed Khoi/Nguni descent indicating that marriages across tribal lines took place.

The earliest contact between the Xhosa and white people was in 1595 when a group of survivors from Santo Alberto, a ship of Portuguese origin, made their way along the coast. It was reported to be an encounter of great kindness and mutual respect.

Today the Xhosa inhabit the Transkei and Ciskei areas on the south-east coast of Southern Africa and many have made their homes in the cities along the coastline. The customs of the traditional Xhosa, however, remain close to their Nguni origins.

Swazi people

The Swazi people, although similar to the Zulu group in their language and culture, were not fighters. The powers of the King were shared with the Queen Mother, resulting in a distinctively balanced system. The blood line of the Swazi royal family can be traced back thirty generations to when their first leaders led them across the Lebombo Mountains to settle in what is now Swaziland.

Although the relationship with their Zulu neighbours was, at times, uneasy, a good bond was established between the two groups when Shaka accepted two of the Swazi ruler's daughters as his wives. A Swazi chief later killed Dingane, resulting in a situation where they had to start defending themselves against the Zulus. They were never great warriors, even though under the leadership of Mswati I many sought their protection. This ensured a fairly secure

environment for their cultural evolution and, in terms of numbers, the nation grew larger,

Relations between the Swazis and whites were initially friendly and peaceful. However, the whites annexed the Swazis' land, imposed taxation and placed the country under British rule. Swaziland became an independent state in 1968.

Ndebele people

The Ndebele people are scattered over three parts of Southern Africa; two of these in the Transvaal (Southern and Northern) and the third in Zimbabwe, once known as Matabeleland. The Ndebele people have spent centuries with the Sothos and have adopted many of their attributes although they are originally from the Nguni tribe. The name Ndebele is derived from the Sotho word for the Nguni. However, prior to the Sotho influence, they lived closely with the Xhosas and the Zulus.

The Zimbabwe Ndebele stem from a Zulu chief and his warriors who fled from Shaka during 1823, settled in Central Transvaal and were then driven north by the Voortrekkers in 1838. The Southern Ndebele retain more of their Nguni origins while the Northern group display a greater Sotho influence.

The Ndebele people are known for their skills in design and decorative, painted murals using natural pigments. My friend Nomvula is from the Northern Transvaal Ndebele tribe.

Sotho tribe

At approximately the same time that the Nguni tribe moved south, the Sotho tribe inhabited the Northern and Eastern Transvaal. They were also cattle keepers although they placed more emphasis on agriculture, hunting, mining and metal-working. The Sotho tribe established themselves in the mountains and adapted to the cold, dry weather conditions.

Tswana people

The Tswana people are also known as the Western Sothos. They suffered tremendously from invasions and were weakened by internal disputes. The Tswana people scattered into about fifty groups and, although they lived together in relatively large groups, the basic family unit has remained similar to that of their cousins, the Nguni. Unlike the Zulus, the Tswanas were not fighters and the larger settlements are believed to have been for defence purposes.

Class distinction is what sets the Tswana apart from other tribes. This started with movement between the tribes and resulted in the classification of three groups; the noble class, the common class and the immigrants. A period of probation was necessary for a person to be accepted while the right to own property was prohibited. Land was generally controlled by the chief and his advisers and each household was allocated a piece of land to cultivate.

The Tswana chiefs were renowned for their mystical ability to make rain and a special courtyard, behind the main wife's hut, was set aside for these rituals. The more successful a chief was with this art, the more popular he became, leading to competition and jealousy.

Responsibility for leadership was that of the chief although each section had its own headman who judged disputes. All headmen, including the chief, had a small group of advisers who helped in the decision making. When an agreement could not be reached all the adult men would be summoned to a public meeting. More of this in Chapter 3.

South Sotho

This group is commonly known as the Basotho and are concentrated in what is now called Lesotho in the South East of Southern Africa (bordering modern Transkei, Orange Free State and KwaZulu Natal). The rise of the Zulu army brought about sudden changes in this relatively peaceful tribe. A young chief, Moshweshwe, led a small

group of refugees into an impregnable fortress on top of the Mountain of the Night (Thaba Bosiu) from where all intruders were beaten off. Various small groups of refugees soon joined his group for protection and within a few years the Basotho state was born with the same young chief as their undisputed leader.

Soon the missionaries arrived bringing with them potential dangers to the Basotho people. The result was a twenty-year tug of war until, finally, in 1868, the rugged hills of Lesotho were returned to the tribe. Independence came in 1966 and today this area is known as the Kingdom of Lesotho, land of extremes. It consists mainly of mountains where people are isolated and traditions are kept alive through lack of outside influence. However, those in the city of Maseru have changed drastically due to its increasingly cosmopolitan nature.

North Sotho

What makes the North Sotho unique is the fact that they are ruled by a Queen. The legendary Rain Queen Mujaji, granddaughter of the famous ruler Monomathapa, was taught the art of rain-making by her mother and given various rain charms and sacred beads. She fled the tribe after giving birth to an illegitimate son and took with her a few loyal supporters.

The small number of modern North Sotho that are her direct descendants are still governing in a hierarchical system ruled by class, with the North Sotho group regarding themselves as one step above other non-Sotho groups. Those wishing to belong to this group both respected and feared her and unanimously accepted her leadership resulting in peaceful assimilation. Permanent changes came with the arrival of the white man and, although their lives are filled with ritual today, much less respect for traditional beliefs is evident among the younger generations. The present Mujaji lives in a royal village situated near the town of Tzaneen in the Lobowa area.

VENDA TRIBE

The Venda tribe is the first of the two smaller groups referred to earlier. The Venda and Lemba tribes are believed to have arrived together in the Northern Transvaal from near Lake Malawi towards the end of the seventeenth century, bringing with them the large bows that earned them the respect of other groups.

Legend has it that the Lemba were descended from a group who had traded with and learned the art of metal work from the Arabs. The Venda on the other hand were particularly skilled in pottery, weaving, basketry and tannery; probably due to the fact that the tsetse fly caused them to find alternative skills to the more traditional African cattle-keeping. Agriculture was another area where they were considered to be superior, cultivating various types of grain and a large variety of vegetables.

Together these two groups constructed furnaces in ant-heaps, melting iron ore to produce small artifacts that became their medium of exchange, compensating for their lack of cattle. This trade died out with the arrival of white people with their cheaply produced metal artifacts, like mass-produced pots and pans.

TSONGA TRIBE

Like most other tribes, the Tsonga was greatly affected by the Zulus and in particular Shaka's warriors. It is uncertain exactly where they originated from but they were living in upper KwaZulu Natal, probably migrating from modern day Mozambique, during the nineteenth century. They moved west and formed their own dynasty when the turmoil of Shaka's days was at its peak. This group is often referred to as the Shangaans.

Although the Tsonga kept cattle and cultivated land, they were particularly skilled in hunting. Fishing was their speciality which included river, dam and sea fishing using hook, line and various traps. They also hunted both small and big game including

ippopotamuses and elephant. Considering the danger involved, pecial magical rituals were required prior to the hunt and a special leansing ritual afterwards.

he Tsonga who remained in what is now Mozambique were traders ho acted as middlemen for the Arab and European traders, eriodically arriving at Delagoa Bay. Ivory and gold were particularly rofitable although they bartered for anything from cloth to copper.

Today's African

he initial contact between the black African and the white uropean was believed by many to have been peaceful and eneficial to both parties. The greatest changes, however, came with he missionaries who brought with them the written word and a new nythology, the Bible. This Pandora's box has been a source of many roblems and great suffering.

hristianity brought a new belief to the people of Southern Africa hich placed the emphasis more on a single God and less on their ncestors. With this new religion came a greater reliance on money ollowed by detribalisation. As new social lifestyles were introduced, nore and more stress was experienced resulting in more illnesses eing treated with modern medicine. All of this created a fast hanging society that was affected on every level.

he mining industry brought new opportunities for men to earn a living nd migrating workers often left their families behind to fend for hemselves. In the past, where a man's position was determined purely y his birth, the new system offered the individual an opportunity to each a new social level, based on material gain. However, this led to reviously peaceful and self-contained communities being destroyed.

outhern Africa with its newly discovered wealth – gold in 1854 and 884, diamonds in 1869 – resulted in conflict as the European owers fought over control of the new wealth. They regarded outhern Africa as the domain of the 'white man' with an endless upply of cheap black labour.

Black women soon followed the men to the cities where they became servants and housekeepers in the homes of white families, resulting in the final collapse of the traditional black family system. Babies that were born in the cities were legally only allowed to stay with their mothers for the first three years of their lives. A child was then sent to its grandmother in the rural areas who assumed the role of both mother and father, while being financially supported by both the parents.

EXERCISE 2
THE CAMP FIRE

This exercise should be done at night when you are out in the country. The ideal situation will present itself and it is therefore recommended not to create it but to wait for the right time.

Build a fire on an open piece of ground with small pieces of wood and let it burn. Once the fire burns strongly, place small pieces of wet wood on to the flames and listen to their crackling sound. Make sure that the area is totally dark and allow the flames to dance and create their own light.

The intention behind this exercise is to connect all five senses to Africa. Once the fire is prepared, find yourself a spot to sit. Try to refrain from sitting on a chair; instead you may wish to sit on a log or a rock. The ideal would be for you to sit flat on the ground with your legs stretched out.

Let your eyes focus on the flames, note their playful dances and then allow them to continue their dance after you have closed your eyes. Be aware of the darkness that surrounds you and create in your mind the image of unseen wild animals lurking behind you, curiously studying your every move. As long as you remain near the fire you will be safe as wild animals are afraid of fire.

Listen to the sound of the fire. Notice how the flames lick across the surface of the wood, creating pressure inside the wet pieces and then popping them as if they contain tiny bubbles.

Incorporate other sounds around you to become part of your experience. In your mind change the sound of traffic to that of a roaring lion and imagine barking dogs as howling hyenas.

Now smell the fire. Breathe in deeply the aromas produced by the wood and allow the smoke to flow over you. Let it inside you and then make it part of yourself. Now taste the resultant flavour in your mouth and imagine you are in dark Africa, sitting by a camp fire.

Allow your fingers to touch the area around you. Feel the different textures that a small handful of sand produces while you rub it between your hands. Let all your senses become aware of the energy of the fire and your surroundings.

FAMILY STRUCTURE

*P*lease note, Africans have become increasingly urbanised and
Westernised and, as a result, the customs, ceremonies and rituals
outlined in this chapter no longer exist in the form described, in the
majority of communities. In certain rural areas, however, some of these
ceremonies and customs remain unchanged.

Staple diets

Africans have lived off the land for many centuries by cultivating the
soil and keeping cattle. Each family produced enough food for their
own needs with their own labour. Although they kept cattle, their
survival depended on agriculture which was taken care of by the
woman in the settlement.

Men seldom helped the woman with these chores and considered it
a favour to assist with heavy tasks. A wooden hoe was used to
cultivate the land and, traditionally, sorghum was planted. Today
the most common crop is maize and the diet is supplemented with
vegetables like pumpkin.

Cattle were highly prized and the kraal was often in the centre of the
village with the houses built in circles around them. Men were
responsible for the cattle, often using these duties as opportunities
to meet and perform exclusively male rituals. Cattle also provided
food in the forms of meat and milk while the cattle hides were used
for clothing and the horns for containers. The cattle dung was used
for fuel and for plastering the walls of their huts. Cattle were

Young woman with child

considered a source of wealth and were used in sacrifices as well as to pay the fathers of their wives-to-be the bridewealth, commonly referred to as Labola.

Friends and neighbours often assisted with the more difficult tasks in exchange for similar help at a later stage. During the time that game was abundant, hunting supplemented the diet. The hunting, however, was undertaken by large groups of men and therefore the whole village would benefit with the kill divided amongst all involved. Hunting was also viewed as a sport, since a family, which often included a number of close relatives such as aunts and uncles, could not support themselves on this alone.

Traditional dress

Traditional dress in most tribes incorporated leather although this is seldomly seen today. Head covering was particularly popular and Xhosa speaking women wore leather caps. Today a simple turban made of cloth is worn in a variety of different ways, often using hat pins as decoration.

Old man in traditional dress

A diviner was often recognised by her beaded hair while her assistant wore a simple head cloth held down by a doughnut-shaped crown of dried grass and a beaded chin strap. The traditional hairstyle of an adult Zulu woman was created by weaving her hair and stretching it over a light wooden frame. This is seldom seen today and has been replaced by a cloth worn wrapped around the head and tied in a knot at the back.

A fascinating tradition was (and still is) practised by the tribal Zulus whereby children of both sexes had their ears pierced and plugged with inserts that were periodically replaced with larger ones. These stretched the earlobes until they could hold a disc, sometimes as big as a saucer. This was believed to 'open' a child's ears, thereby helping them to learn and understand better.

Unmarried women in many of the African tribes were recognised by their naked breasts while some tribes wore feathers in their hair to elaborate their status. Amongst the Swazi people, a red feather in the hair of both male and female indicated royal blood.

Grass hoops worn from the top of their necks to the bottom of their legs were worn by the Ndebele woman during rituals. These awkward hoops were accompanied by elaborate beadwork in the form of an apron and head covering. The Ndebele are known for

their colourfully painted homes, and this artistic gift is used to its fullest in their traditional outfits.

The origin of these hoops is believed to date back to the times of tribal war when, in the heat of an attack, the women ran away, leaving the men to fight the battle and take care of the children. This caused great difficulties for the men and the hoops were introduced to limit the movement of the women, slowing them down and enabling the men to catch up with them and return them to the settlement. Many women still wear brass hoops around their necks and legs, resulting in particularly long necks and calves.

In recent years, some Swazi tribes have shown signs of returning to their traditional ways of dressing. The women wear a beehive hairstyle that is covered with a black net and is kept in place by a simple string of white beads. This hairstyle is protected by a chiffon cloth during their day-to-day activities.

Another tradition, maintained by the Tsonga women, is their hip-flicking dance. They exaggerate these movements by wearing extravagantly gathered double-layered skirts made from approximately 60 metres of cotton material. These skirts are expensive and are, therefore, passed on from mother to daughter. The outer appearance is changed by wearing different cloths tied over the shoulder and draped over the skirt, creating a bulky dress.

Missionaries during the nineteenth century had a strong influence on certain tribes. This is clearly evident amongst the Pedi (of Sotho origin) ladies in their gathered skirts with their pin-tucks and frills. The traditional skirts, from before the missionary influence, are still worn by some women albeit with a more Western appearance.

Settlements

The Nguni built huts in circles and semi-circles around the kraal, while the Sotho surrounded their homestead with cattle kraals. The early Nguni and Sotho huts were grass-thatched using a frame of bent saplings while the Tsonga and Venda used stakes. The general method was to build a frame using two rows of wooden stakes several feet apart. This created a cavity which was filled with rocks, stones and soil while tall grass was used to thatch the roof. Cattle dung was then used to plaster the walls and floor.

Typical Swazi hut   Typical Zulu beehive hut

Settlement patterns varied: the Nguni and Tshonga lived in small scattered groups; the Sotho and Venda lived in large villages. These settlements were situated on slopes or ridges with a level area for cultivation.

Strict rules were applied in the layout of these settlements and the position of a hut was determined by the status a person held in the community. The chief's wife's hut was in the central position while the huts of the other wives were set alongside according to their status. Each wife had her own sleeping hut that she shared with her young children while the other boys and girls shared separate huts.

There was a kitchen hut, guest hut, granny hut and storage hut. The kitchen hut was probably the busiest and noisiest spot in any settlement as this was where all meals were prepared by the women. While the maize was pounded into meal before preparing it as porridge, the women were surrounded by their young, chatting and swopping advice.

Typical Xhosa homestead

Probably the most sociable period was at meal time around the evening fires when the bigger children moved from fire to fire, eating as they went. Boys in particular were sociable and enjoyed their time at home with their friends, especially after having been away herding cattle all day. After the meal the men were the first to retire to their beds, leaving the women telling stories about times gone by. Oral tradition remains an important part of rural people's lives.

Riddles were popular, especially around the fire after the evening meal. An example of such a riddle would be: 'What is the thing that once poured out cannot be gathered?' to which the answer is 'Water'. Another is: 'Who am I if my relatives are numerous?' The answer is 'A star'. These riddles were a highlight for the children and probably created a strong bond between the grandmothers and the children.

GROWING UP

Children brought up within this extended family had a different life from the Westerner. Most importantly a child's status depended on its birth, i.e. the status of the mother within the homestead.

Education was designed to prepare the child for its future position within the group rather than developing individual talents. The task of educating the youngsters was shared by all members of the family, including aunts, uncles and cousins. The youngsters learned by imitating the older members of the clan.

Young boy   Young girl

During their early years children travelled on the mother's back and were breast fed on demand until well over a year old. Seldom did one see a young child wearing anything other than a simple string of beads. They later spent their days playing, singing and dancing with the older children, while they remained safe in the warm environment where almost every adult was a relative.

At around five or six years old, the sexes were separated with the girls helping around the homestead to take care of younger children, fetch water, grind corn and cook while the boys explored the environment and herded cattle with the older boys. Here they spent their time dreaming about becoming great warriors and, at times, spent weeks away from the settlement.

A tradition maintained by a number of tribes was that of keeping a miniature village where youngsters could play adult games. These games included parenting whereby young girls would 'borrow'

younger siblings to act as children whilst the young men would borrow their father's tools to construct huts. They would build a settlement from scratch and while doing so, would imitate the behaviour of their parents. Once all the lessons were learned, the miniature settlement would be destroyed, leaving an empty space, until another group of children were ready to start again.

Puberty

An ancient belief is attached to circumcision, and marking the transition from a child to an adult, that all children are born with both sexes and, at puberty, one sex is removed by cutting away part of the genitals and scarring the face.

Although one still hears horrific stories of female mutilation in todays society, circumcision of girls is rarely practised. Normally, at the first menstruation, a girl would be secluded from all activities for up to six days. During this time the Venda and the North Sotho girl suffered greatly, beaten by the older girls and given poor food. This was believed to be good discipline that would assist her in married life. A final cleansing ritual ended her days of childhood and she emerged as a woman from the hut.

The initiation of boys marked the change of status from childhood to adulthood and varied from group to group. The general idea was to remove the initiates from society for a period (up to six months), accommodating them in a specially built initiation hut, usually in a secluded area. This period was considered one of the major events in a young man's life and at times involved a long wait since these rituals took place every two to twelve years.

The initiation began with a ritual meal, after which the initiates discarded their clothes and put on a blanket. They were then taken to a river where the circumcision was performed. It was important for the boy not to show any fear or pain as this would bring shame to him and his family. The foreskins were buried in an anthill where the termites destroyed them to prevent sorcerers from using them.

Young men on their way to the river

After circumcision the young boys were smeared with mud and taken back to the hut where they remained until their wounds had healed. During this period they were taught about sexual behaviour and were only allowed to eat maize prepared by their guardians. Once their wounds had healed, an animal was slaughtered and after a ritual meal, the young men once again smeared themselves with clay and paraded through the village. Amongst the South Sotho the young men were given a final beating in a cave before making their passage into manhood.

The end of this initiation was normally marked by the initiates washing themselves in a river and smearing themselves with fat. They then left their hut and, without looking back, walked towards the village while the initiation hut and all its contents were burnt. Amongst the Xhosa people, the young men were given new names to replace their childhood names. The whole initiation period could last anything from three to six months.

Adult Life and Marriage

Once they returned to the homestead, they could no longer share their mother's hut. Young people were given sexual freedom after initiation

although young men were discouraged from deflowering a girl. Anal sex and masturbation were amongst the methods used to maintain this status quo. When, and if this freedom was abused, a fine in the form of a specified number of cattle was due to the respective parents.

In their late teens or early twenties the subject of marriage would generally be raised by the young men. Young couples courted each other by exchanging gifts of beads whereby the colours of the beads carried a special message.

Marriage between relatives was totally forbidden amongst the Nguni but encouraged by the Sotho resulting in a fundamental difference in their community structures.

Marriage, more often than not, was arranged by the parents of the groom. Once the parents of the girl had agreed to the union, the 'labola' (dowry or bridewealth) was negotiated. This consisted mainly of cattle and the amount varied according to the status of the bride's family. When the negotiations started one animal was handed over by the groom to the parents of the bride as a token of goodwill and the rest were presented once the marriage was consummated. This ensured certain rights, most importantly that any children produced by the marriage belonged legally to the groom's family.

However, the bride's family were able to demand more cattle once a child was born and if the bride died. This practice is seen by modern black Africans as an excuse for cheap labour, placing both families in bondage.

Traditional weddings are rare and the couples normally choose a simpler method such as elopement or abduction of the bride by friends of the groom.

Most weddings started with a ritual where an animal was slaughtered before the bride left her home. Once the bride and groom, accompanied by friends, arrived at his homestead, the festivities continued. During this time they would be accommodated in the guest hut and the marriage consummated. Throughout the ritual, the bride was expected to show reluctance and sadness and any sign of joy was frowned upon by the elders as she was about to go and live amongst strangers.

There were many rules that a new bride had to abide by in her new environment. She was not allowed to walk across the meeting place and when moving from hut to hut, she had to use the back entrance. She had to avoid using the names of members of her husband's family and keep her head covered when in their presence. Her first duty was towards her new husband and while she took care of his needs, she was not allowed to drink nor touch any drinking utensils. A final ritual killing marked her acceptance after which she could drink in her husband's homestead but no longer in her father's home.

The new bride was placed in an awkward position as she had few rights during the initial period of marriage. This at times led to abuse, especially when polygamy was a way of life. Polygamy in the old days was an accepted way of life as every woman had to grow enough food for her own offspring and therefore did not burden the man. Today the man has to provide for all his wives and children, resulting in widespread poverty and malnutrition.

After all formalities and festivities had taken place, the new wife was given her own sleeping hut in her husband's homestead. The position of the hut obviously depended on her status while the land to be cultivated depended on the number of dependants within this hut. Each hut operated independently from the others and although cooking facilities were shared, each woman had to provide for her own offspring. Children were highly prized and fertility was crucial to a woman's status in the group.

Death

In the tribal setting, events affecting one person were felt by the whole community and discussed at great length around the fire. Death was one such aspect and, when a person died, the mother (or wife) of the deceased sat on the floor in an empty room while the villagers paid their respects. This routine was therapeutic as the incidents leading up to the death were repeated over and over in great detail. In doing so, the mother (or wife) spoke freely about the death and her feelings, thus accepting the death before the burial.

The deeper beliefs about death are discussed in Chapter 3.

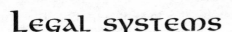

LEGAL SYSTEMS

As in any community where large groups of people live together, sharing the land, disputes often occurred. In order to resolve these disagreements, a system was set in place that, although not as clearly defined as Western legal systems, corresponded in the broad sense of the word, closely to them. Civil cases concerning the rights of individuals were rectified by compensation while criminal cases were punished by means of fines or even death.

Due to their different cultural heritages, what is wrong in the eyes of a Westerner may not even invite a reaction from an African, while the offended African may find the Western system of justice completely inadequate.

A chief in his traditional dress

The people of the Xhosa tribe are well known for the passion they mostly demonstrated during public hearings, arguing with their sharp minds and tackling the problem from every conceivable point of view. These disputes could take days to resolve during to-and-fro haggling. Land was often disputed, inch by inch, in a tug of war that may only have been concluded years after the initial hearing. The chief made the final decision and if no agreement could be reached a settlement was offered. Should this not be accepted, the case would go to an appeal court where the whole argument would be repeated.

EXERCISE 3
THE RAIN DANCE

Rain is the most important factor in tribal African life, whether farming cattle or crops. The areas discussed in this chapter have, under normal circumstances, a reasonably high rainfall in the summer months. Winter is relatively short, stretching from May to August, during which sub-zero temperatures can be recorded. During summer, however, temperatures can reach up to 40° Celsius, creating stifling heat and discomfort.

Find yourself a patch of grass outside during a cloudy day and lie down. Allow your eyes to scan the sky for hidden pictures in the clouds and see how they slowly change shape. Allow your intuition to flow through your imagination and notice how these figures interact with each other, and slowly let the story unfold itself. Become aware of the heat of the sun when the clouds move away and feel the perspiration on the surface of your skin.

Now notice how the clouds blend and become heavier until finally the tiny little drops held within are too heavy to remain there. They leave the safety of the sky and tumble towards you, soaking into your clothing and the grass around you. Get back on to your feet and start dancing with joy. Feel the happiness within you as a tiny seed that can now, with the nourishment of the rain, grow into a strong beautiful plant producing food during hungry days. Allow this feeling to grow even during dry days and keep watering it during rainy days. It will serve you well.

3 AFRICAN BELIEFS

In this chapter we will look at some of the most common beliefs, irrespective of whether they are myths, legends or historical facts. African legends claim to have larger-than-life heroes while the folktales tell of talking animals and monsters, not unlike the stories young children are told in the Western world.

The CREATOR

Probably the most common element shared by the various tribes is their belief in a superior being who was responsible for the creation. To tell all the stories related to this would fill many pages and is not the purpose of this book. What is important is the fact that all tribes believe in a superior being which I will call God. There appears to be a lot of confusion as to where God actually came from.

One story tells of how God sent a chameleon to inspect the creation and to convey a message of eternal life to humankind. The chameleon took its time so God became impatient and sent a lizard to announce human mortality. Both these animals are prominent in African mythology.

Once the creation was completed, God withdrew His support, showing little interest in humans' day-to-day life. The reason for this withdrawal was that humans made so many demands on God that He grew tired and angry. It is said that the early Mende people in Sierra Leone thought God's name was 'Take it!' as they heard this every time a demand was made.

God made Himself a home far away and above humans and one night while the humans were asleep, God moved. When humans woke up, they saw God spread in all directions. He was no longer actively involved in their affairs. He was from then on referred to as the God in the sky.

In order for living beings to reach God, ancestors and nature spirits were used as go betweens. This has often been interpreted by Western society as making gods and idols out of ancestors, which is not necessarily true. Spirits of the dead are important in Africa as is belief in life after death. God, however is an abstract idea, believed to be 'too great to be contained in a house', which probably explains the absence of temples to God.

God is benevolent, cares for humans and does not strike them with terror. He lives in heaven and is particularly concerned with rain, upon which humans depend for their survival. God is rarely associated with the sun. Some groups believe God is one of twins, one of whom is associated with the sun while the other is connected with the moon.

Rain-making was an important function practised by the chiefs of the Tswana tribe and they each had a special rain-making enclosure behind the main wife's hut. A chief's popularity depended greatly on his success with these rites which were practised at the beginning of every agricultural season. The North Sotho had a Queen with these special rain-making powers. An ability to make rain indicated to the people that the chief was in direct contact with God.

Death

There are many myths associated with Death and the common factor amongst all tribes is that death has a personality and needs to be eliminated. As mentioned earlier in this chapter, immortality was believed by some to have been brought by a chameleon who was overtaken by the lizard carrying the message of death. The general belief is that death is not natural and is always caused by another force. Death therefore has to be fought and the 'best man' will win.

A distinction is made between the body of a person and that which is contained within the body. This, in Western terms, relates to the soul but is referred to as the *moya*, meaning wind and breath. When a person dies, the breath or wind leaves the body. There is little speculation as to what happens to this breath energy after death.

In addition to the *moya* each living person also has a shadow or *isithunsi*. The shadow of a person contains the qualities presented to the world and the closest association in Western culture is probably the personality. When a person dies, the shadow is lost, which is far more significant than the loss of breath. Chiefs, warriors and diviners may have more than one shadow or a larger shadow than the average and therefore, once deceased, become powerful ancestors with strong influence in the spiritual realm.

Ancestral spirits

Nothing in African culture happens by accident and every incident is investigated for its cause. Bad luck simply does not exist and when bad things happen to someone, the cause is often found to have originated from either witchcraft or ancestral interference. This is probably the most common thread that runs through African cultures.

With God not actively involved in the day-to-day life of humans, the spirits or shadows of the recently departed ancestors, such as parents and grandparents, act as go-betweens. Great grandparents are seldom recognised. This is an important, fundamental spiritual belief that is practised by almost all the tribes in Southern Africa. The Tswana are one of the few groups that no longer practise ancestral rituals.

Not every spirit falls into the category of the ancestral spirits. A child, for instance, is believed to join the forefathers but not as a go-between. A special ceremony is held one to two years after the funeral to change the status of the departed spirit. During this ritual an ox is slaughtered and the best meat is offered to the ancestors, calling them by name. This will be the first time that the name of the recently deceased person is included amongst those of the long-departed ancestors. The spirit is then asked to return home in order to help the living while the eldest living son then draws a path, using a branch, from the grave to the main hut in the settlement. This is to help the spirit find its way back.

The spirit of an ancestor is unpredictable and holds the power to help or to harm descendants. It is therefore important not to upset these spirits. Ancestors communicate with the living through their dreams, offering them instruction or expressing their grievances. Offering of beer and the sacrifice of animals are used during times of crisis to ensure their assistance.

Ancestral influence is generally accredited to instances when a fortunate incident occurs or when a persisting illness is contracted. (More of this in Chapter 4.) Ancestral spirits played a particularly important role as far as crops were concerned and many sacrifices were made prior to the rainy season to ensure that food was plentiful. Another important role was that of protection when individuals were away from home. Warriors and hunters praised their ancestors when they returned safely from a period away.

The Princess of Heaven

The Zulu tribe believed that the God who lives in the sky had a daughter, referred to as the Princess of Heaven. She was predominantly responsible for the fertility of humans and beasts and announced her presence with mists and rainbows. She was believed to have been a naked virgin with buttocks of fire and any man that gazed upon her would become ill and die.

Prior to the agricultural season, young girls borrowed the clothes of their brothers, including their shields and sticks and took a bull and a cow to be herded. The cow was left under a tree with two of the girls while the bull was led away by the remainder up the hill where an offering was made to the Princess of Heaven. This offering included a special beer and the seeds of various plants.

The girls sang and danced and called upon the Princess for her assistance in providing for a good harvest and for faithful hearts in their lovers. It was important that no man or boy should partake in

this ritual as the songs sung apparently described explicit sexual matters. Any curious onlookers were chased away.

Snakes

Snakes hold a fascination for people from many cultures. Some African tribes believe that the snake was made before the universe was created and that God travelled in its mouth. Snakes, of which the python is a favourite, are believed to be immortal because they shed their skin but continue to live. When swallowing its own tail, the snake becomes the symbol of eternity, and this is often depicted in art.

Another story tells of a dog that was instructed by God to take new skins to the first humans in order that they might renew themselves. On its way, the dog stopped to eat and when asked what the bag contained, it told its host the story. A snake overheard this and sneaked up on the dog and stole the skins. Man was thereafter no longer immortal while the snake, even though in exile, could shed its skin and renew itself.

Masks and drums

Masks and drums were important in all ceremonies. Both of these were made from wood. Masks modelled on animal faces were popular as they were believed to concentrate the power associated with the particular animal in the head while wearing the mask. The wearer would be protected from evil for the duration of the ceremony by the powers of that particular animal.

Drums, on the other hand, created not only a sound to accompany the dance but also brought forth the energy of the object that was carved on to its side.

Both masks and drums were important items that were used by the early Africans to express their interpretations of life. These were employed in every aspect of life, including religion, creating their own unique 'temples' to celebrate God's presence.

Young women dancing

EXERCISE 4
TRANCE DANCE

Drums are, as mentioned before, an essential instrument to accompany dancing during a ceremony. In Western culture, dancing is also appreciated for its therapeutic value and the intention behind this exercise is to help you experience this phenomenon in an African way.

Find a room in which you can safely dance without injuring yourself. Cover your eyes with a scarf and plug your ears with cottonwool. It may be advisable to have another person to act as your eyes for this brief period and to prevent you from bumping into things. Another way to do this is to find an erect object such as a washing-line pole and to tie yourself to it with a thin rope. It will certainly stop you from bumping into other objects. In a group setting, this exercise becomes very powerful.

Concentrate all your awareness inside your body and become aware of your heartbeat. Feel the heart contracting its muscles and then pushing the blood into your veins, echoing the sound through your whole body. Concentrate on hearing your heartbeat as it pushes the blood into the tiny veins in your ears and feel the same in your tongue. Become aware how your whole body pulses with the rhythm of your heartbeat, while the blood rushes through your veins.

Slowly start walking in a circle with every step mirroring every heartbeat. Let the rhythm take you deeper within yourself and imagine the sounds inside your body. Hear the drums beat and imagine that the blood flows on command of the drum. Notice the almost electrical silences between each rush, the anticipation of the next.

Gradually, as your muscles demand more oxygen, your heartbeat is increased and the oxygen-rich blood rushes through your veins. The rhythm is increasing and you are moving faster while the sound is getting louder. Feel yourself entering a new dimension, untouched by the conscious mind: a space that exists within you, occupied by your higher self and silently present wherever you go. Mechanisms that are controlled by your Creator, sustaining your whole physical being.

Feel the energy as oxygen enters your body through your breath into your lungs where it is transformed. Become aware of the intricate processes taking place within your body and keep your awareness with the inner world.

Allow the trance to continue for as long as you wish, then slowly reverse the process by shifting your awareness to the outer world until your conscious mind is back in control.

4

WITCHCRAFT
AND SORCERY

The whole belief system of witchcraft and sorcery is really to protect the ancestors from evil. God is not actively involved in human lives and therefore cannot be blamed for misfortune.

There are different types of misfortunes and it is important to be able to distinguish between them. The first distinction needs to be made between an illness or misfortune that is brought about by the ancestors and one that originates from witchcraft. Although the illnesses may be similar, the prescribed medication or cure is indeed different.

The first type of illness is caused by the ancestors and is discussed in Chapter 5 while the second type is brought about by others, either intentionally or unintentionally. The important fact concerning the latter, is that the cause is from an outside influence and the sufferer is not able to heal the disease. Both these situations will be diagnosed by a diviner although there are different solutions to both problems.

Misfortunes caused by others can be initiated, first through the use of inherited mystical powers or second with the use of herbs and medicine. Anthropologists refer to the first as witchcraft and the second as sorcery. When a misfortune happens by 'accident', it is referred to as pollution. Although the symptoms of a victim may be identical for all the above categories, the cures vary profoundly.

Most tribes distinguish between witches and sorcerers by calling them 'day witches' (mystical – women) and 'night witches (medicinal – men). The fact is, no witch or sorcerer is physically recognisable, creating the need for the diviner, discussed in Chapter 5.

WITCHCRAFT

Witchcraft was, and still is, practised mainly by women with a mystical ability. Usually hereditary in nature, it is said to have enabled some of them to change shape, become invisible or to send agents (referred to as 'familiars' by anthropologists) to do their evil work. A real witch was believed to have magical powers that enabled her to fly through the air and enter a house through a crack. Victims were often removed from their beds while asleep and taken to the bush where they were beaten, waking up with bruised bodies followed by either a miscarriage or failed crops.

The Tsonga and Venda tribes believed that a witch was normal during the day and that her witch spirit would leave her sleeping body at night to perform evil deeds. She was therefore not consciously aware of her powers. The Nguni and Sotho, however, believed her to be in total control of these actions. Whether conscious or not, all witches worked at night, went naked, killed babies, ate human flesh and harmed those close to them.

Although they worked alone, they met secretly at night for sexual engagements. Jealousy was often believed to be the cause of vicious fights during these secretive meetings and they often ended in death.

FAMILIARS

Most common amongst witches was the use of familiars to do their work. These tended to be small animals, such as cats, owls and snakes that could become invisible as well as change their shape. These animals were cared for by the witches and normally fed porridge, milk and meat, although it is known that some familiars at times requested human blood. Such a request was taken seriously as these animals could turn on their keepers.

The best-known familiar is called the *Thikoloshe* and is kept in a hut by the witches and used as a sexual partner. The Xhosas believe him to be a short hairy man with one buttock and an enormous penis. He is believed to be knee-high and is always blamed when a woman loses interest in sex. He is also often believed to be encountered by the young herdboys when he steals milk from the cows.

The *Impundulu* is probably the most feared familiar amongst the Nguni. He is a lightning bird, associated with thunder and lightning, causing death to people and beasts, and failing crops. He is blamed when lightning strikes, and is thought to suck blood from his victims, causing illnesses in the chest area. He could, like most familiars, appear in the form of a handsome man and have intercourse with the witch.

Isithunzela is a familiar that is supposedly a corpse dug from its grave and controlled by witches to do evil deeds. These 'zombies' are also used to cultivate the land of the witches, saving them from performing this heavy task.

SORCERY

As mentioned before, sorcerers are generally men who do their evil deeds through medicine, herbs or spells. They are unable to change their form or become invisible, although they can drop their medicine anywhere. They often use the nail clippings and hair of the victim they wish to harm. This is the main reason why the foreskins after circumcision and the afterbirth are buried in an anthill to be destroyed, saving them from being used by the sorcerers.

A sorcerer does not need part of the body to single out his victim. He can chew the medicine, spit it out, call the person's name and the spell will be cast. Another method was to roast the medicine while boiling water. A finger touched the roasted medicine while a spear was dipped into the boiling water, after which the finger touched the lips while the name was spoken and the spear hurled at a wall. Once the spear touched the ground, the victim started feeling ill.

Familiars are sometimes used by sorcerers and are obtainable from herbalists. One such familiar is the *Umamlambo*. It is a charm that is said to change form – from almost anything to almost anything. It

is believed that when it takes the shape of a snake, any person that looks at it will die unless treated.

PROTECTION

Prevention is better than cure, even in the darkest parts of Africa and protection against witchcraft is practised by most. Witches can work over only a short distance and if necessary, one can always relocate to avoid further attack. However, the most basic method is to protect the settlement from witchcraft by using the services of a herbalist.

Medicine is placed around the border of the settlement, sometimes on wooden pegs driven into the ground, or between huts creating an invisible net to catch the familiars when they try to enter a hut. Herbs are burned inside the huts, driving out any invisible familiars while the inhabitants are cut and herbs rubbed into the wounds.

The Sotho believe that when cold urine is poured over a familiar, it dies. In addition to this, urine weakens the strength of harmful medicine. If it is sprinkled around the border of a settlement, the witches mistake the area for a dam and avoid it.

Although a settlement may be protected against witches and sorcerers, a person is believed to be in danger when away from home and in cases like this, personal charms are used. Ancestral protection is also particularly active when travelling.

ELIMINATION

As mentioned before, nothing in Africa happens by accident and in order to eliminate witches and sorcerers, they first have to be identified by the diviner. They are hated and, when they are discovered, the reaction of the tribe is often violent. They are seen as the opposite of good, the reversal of everything that is normal to human behaviour, thereby upsetting the harmony in nature.

The crimes committed by these people are considered as chief capital crimes. The guilty parties are generally tried in public and the whole family sentenced to death. Amongst the Nguni, the execution is done by pegging a person down, covering the body with water and honey, and then breaking open a nest of vicious black ants. The person is bitten to death while the rest of the family is set alight in their respective huts, thereby eliminating the evil bloodline.

The chief becomes the legal owner of all the possessions of the executed person. This rule at times leads to accusations made against an innocent person who owns a particularly large herd of cattle, resulting in gain for the accuser. It is frightening to think that where normal emotions such as envy and jealousy are present, individuals can be accused of deeds that may result in violent punishment and the destruction of entire families.

Amongst the Nguni, a new daughter-in-law is almost always the first person accused of witchcraft when someone falls ill. This removes the blame from families within the homestead and, instead, casts it outside the ranks of the tribe. Another common phenomenon is accusations between co-wives in polygamous families as each wife has to provide for her own offspring and jealousy is rampant.

The fact that the Sotho and Venda encourage cousins to marry, is probably why accusations are seldom made against a new wife as the guilty party is likely to be of the same bloodline and this may have resulted in the death of the accuser. These tribes appear to fear sorcery far more than witchcraft.

POLLUTION

Pollution is a term used when a person is contaminated through no fault of his or her own. These polluted states are mystical and can be dangerous and should, therefore, be rectified as soon as possible. This is done by performing a purification ritual. There are different levels of pollution and the severity changes from level to level.

The Venda have a limited belief in pollution and perform purification rituals at birth, after the birth of twins, abortion, illness, crime, and burial while the Tsonga include the menstrual flow in their rites. These rituals generally incorporate the burning of medicine, cutting of nails and hair and washing in rivers.

The birth of twins was at one time considered as pollution and the second-born was put to death and buried in damp soil, after which the mother was purified. The birth of twins was considered to affect the universe adversely and could cause a drought. A miscarriage and an abortion were two very sensitive issues as they prevented another individual from being born. These were dealt with by burying the foetus near a river with reeds tied around the four limbs.

A man became impotent if he had sexual intercourse with a woman who was polluted while a woman of childbearing years would become infertile after contact with a polluted man. No polluted person was allowed to touch drinking utensils, medicine and the cattle kraal had to be avoided at all costs as the cattle could lose their fertility.

Pollution was often referred to as having 'heat' and almost all the treatments incorporated the use of water. This condition was also believed to be particularly harsh on the water flow, which obviously affected the crops and thereby the survival of the tribe.

EXERCISE 5
ANCESTRAL STARS

In Western traditions the belief in past lives and spiritual guides is fairly common. It is the opinion of the author that this belief is the same as the African ancestral belief and the intention of this exercise is to connect these two belief systems.

It is stated in the Bible that the sins of the fathers will be repeated even on to the fourth generation, meaning that you will pay for the sins committed by your great grandfather. For the reader comfortable with reincarnation, this would mean that you were your own great grandfather and that you are therefore paying your own karmic debt from the previous incarnation. A deceased relative may also become a spiritual guide that offers guidance from the spiritual dimension.

Find a soft patch of grass outside during a cloudless night and make yourself comfortable. By choosing to do this exercise during a new moon, the reader will experience particularly bright stars. Close your eyes for a brief moment, take a few deep breaths and relax your whole body, from the toes to the scalp. Create in your mind the feelings of a newborn baby, about to open its eyes and look upon the world for the first time.

Now open your eyes and look at the stars. Imagine them to be loving members of your family, some still alive and others long gone to the other side. See the unique way the stars twinkle and imagine the meaning of this. Pay particular attention to any falling or shooting stars as these hold a special meaning.

Ask whatever questions you need to ask and then wait for the reply. Feel the answer in the area behind your navel and then let your mind analyse it. Play around with this and ask for confirmation from the stars. They are there to guide and protect you.

5

AFRICAN DIVINATION

health

*W*hen someone fell ill, the person first tried to solve the problem
with a personal selection of medicine. Failing this, the whole
family made the decision to consult a healer in order to find the cure
and the reasons for the illness. The connections were made to either
witchcraft, ancestral spirits or pollution.

An illness brought on by an ancestral spirit indicated to the sufferer
that his or her duties were not being fulfilled. The victim was
therefore the indirect cause of his or her own disease and healing
took place as soon as the situation was rectified. These conditions
are similar to psychosomatic illnesses encountered in Western
society, where the emotional state is often the cause for the physical
manifestation of the illness.

Correct diagnosis was critical and was done by someone with a
direct link to the ancestral spirits, such as a diviner, while the
dispensing of medication was done by a herbalist. In the Zulu
language, a diviner is called a *Sangoma*, while a herbalist is called
an *Inyanga*. Any person can learn to become an Inyanga, while to
become a Sangoma one must have a calling. These two professions
can be compared to a pharmacist and doctor, respectively.

The calling

Diviners are generally women called to their profession by their ancestors. This normally happens, as discussed earlier, when an illness cannot be healed or a misfortune cannot be explained by any means other than that of a diviner who diagnoses the calling. The type of illness is generally stomach-ache or painful joints that result in a disturbed sleeping pattern accompanied by restless dreams.

The dreams normally include an animal that contains the spirit of an ancestor. Zulus associate snakes with ancestral spirits while the Vendas recognise the spirit of a departed chief in a lion. These animals appear in the dream with a message indicating that the calling has been made.

Confirmation of the calling is made by a Sangoma who often recognises this by the reluctance in the 'patient'. Should a person choose not to take up the calling, the illness will get worse and may result in madness or even death. The only escape is to take up the challenge.

The apprenticeship

The diviner who identifies the cause of the illness normally takes the student under her wing. From a cynical point of view, a vulnerable person can easily be manipulated into this situation, as much money is at stake. An apprenticeship can cost a great deal of money, and even though the period of learning depends mainly on the abilities of the pupil, most students qualify at the end of two to three years.

The student lives a lonely life under the same roof as her teacher, constantly fearing pollution as this will have a negative effect on her healing powers. During this period, she is not allowed to shake hands with anyone younger than herself and she must avoid the shadows of others touching her. The food that she is allowed to eat is dictated to her by the ancestors through the teacher. Her head is shaved and she is allowed only simple clothing with her head covered in a manner similar to that of a newly wed.

During these years, the student is totally at the mercy of her teacher and the ancestors. She accompanies her teacher to wherever the patients are and also collects herbs, roots and other materials to make medicine, referred to as *muti*.

The original illness is cured during the period of the apprenticeship mainly through ritual killings, dream confession and trance dancing. The trance dance is mainly a channel for the ancestors to communicate through the apprentice and it is also considered to have a strong healing effect. This therapy is particularly effective when there are many people clapping their hands during the dance.

An important task during this time is for the student to start collecting her own set of 'bones'. This consists of various objects that have symbolic value to the apprentice and can only be collected by her. A detailed description of these will follow in Chapter 6.

The student is tested periodically during the apprenticeship by the teacher. One such test is for the teacher to throw the bones into a pot containing beer and then ask the student to interpret the way that they have fallen. A psychic ability is of great advantage although it is still believed that the ancestors provide the answers.

Once a teacher is satisfied with the abilities of her student, an initiation ceremony is arranged and the student graduates.

The initiation

There are four important steps in the initiation process of a Sangoma, the first of which is probably the most dangerous. The initiate is called to the river by the 'river-people' who are believed to live in beautiful homes at the bottom of the river where they hold a special gift for her to make her own.

The initiate walks into the river and sinks to the bottom where she then collects the gift, while a group herding cattle on the bank is on stand-by to ensure her safe return. Sending cattle into the river is believed to be the only way to save her from the snakes that may attack her while under water. Some initiates do not survive this part of the process as the rivers in rural areas can be crocodile infested.

The second part requires a goat to be slaughtered and the meat to be boiled with *muti* in a pot that contains the bones of an initiate. The resulting broth is then drunk by the initiate, creating a blood bond that connects her with the goat and the bones. Sometimes she will be expected to drink the blood of the animal after the bones and *muti* have been soaked for a certain period of time. Today, away from the informal settlements of the past, chickens have replaced the goat for sacrificial purposes as limited space is available in the townships of modern South Africa.

The initiate is given muti during the third stage of the process. The *muti* contains the eyes and nose (symbolising sight and smell) of a wild animal such as a vulture or wild cat. This is no longer possible in urban areas due to the lack of such wild animals and the eyes and noses of the animal that has been slaughtered may be used instead. The eyes of a cat can see in darkness, giving the Sangoma the ability to see the invisible, while extra sense of smell will assist her to smell out any witches and sorcerers.

The fourth and final step is to bury the bones of the animal that has been slaughtered at a crossroad near the settlement. This is done secretively at night to prevent competitive Sangomas from removing these for their own use. The symbolism behind this is for the animal to watch the movement of people and pass this information through the bond created during the earlier phases of initiation.

The student is now a fully qualified Sangoma and a celebration is held inviting all the neighbours to join in the success. She can now find her own patients and work independently from her teacher.

Divination

The success of a Sangoma depends very much on her accurate interpretation of her set of bones, which we will discuss in Chapter 6. The higher the regard for her insight, the quicker the execution of an identified witch. There have been cases where a person has been pointed out and without being given an opportunity to defend herself,

was subsequently put to death. Generally, a person will get a second and third opinion on serious matters such as this.

The patient plays an important role in the consultation, clapping their hands and making statements that either confirm or deny what is said, helping the Sangoma to assess her insight. The terms *Siyavuma* (meaning 'We agree') when she is correct and *Asiva* (meaning 'We do not hear') when she is wrong are commonly used. This helps her establish whether she is on the right track or not. If the patient is not happy with too many Asivas, they simply take their money and go to someone else.

Diagnosis

To be a Sangoma or an Inyanga confers the immediate respect of the whole community. Families, together, make the decision to consult them as the reason behind illness often involves the whole family. They deal with this as a group and only once the cause of the illness is fully understood, can the healing take place.

In the case of sorcery or witchcraft against a person, a Sangoma may suggest that the guilty party is, for example, 'an overweight, old woman who lives diagonally across from you'. This often leads to false accusations as a person of this description can be found in any town or city. Never is a specific name used to identify a guilty party.

Medicine

Medicine is referred to as *muti* and is mainly of vegetable origin, although animal dung is sometimes included. Flesh or fat from an animal (or even human) is often used in a manipulative and destructive way, as is done by sorcerers.

The core of African medicine lies in association, i.e. linking the qualities of the plant or animal with the need in the patient. An example of this is the eyes and nose of the animal slaughtered during the initiation and the connected belief that this will increase the sight and smell of the diviner. Medicines dispensed for psychosomatic complaints probably have an effect merely due to the belief of the patient, while others have proved to work over many centuries.

Muti is not always prescribed as many illnesses call for a sacrifice that usually requires an animal to be slaughtered, especially when an ancestral spirit has expressed his displeasure at a patient. A child's cough is cured by tying a key around his neck, 'locking in' the cough, while pig fat provides protection against snake bites.

Muti is taken orally, inhaled, bathed in, rubbed on and applied in every other conceivable way possible.

EXERCISE 6
THE MOON AND WEATHER

The moon is directly responsible for the movement of water on the planet, such as high and low tide, thus emotions are linked to water. As mentioned previously, water is an important commodity in Africa and it therefore gives the moon mystical powers connected with rain.

Rain-makers used to study various factors in nature and soon the pattern of rain was established. When the signs of expected rain were clear, a rain dance was performed. The clearer the interpretations of the natural aspects, the more urgent the dance ceremony, resulting in an almost magical belief in the chief and his powers.

Learning to read the signs of promised rain is easy and can be done by almost anyone, anywhere. Use a period from full moon to full moon during the rainy season and record the appearance of the moon preferably at the same time every night. Particular attention should be paid to the shape of the moon, its relation to the four cardinal points (north, east, south and west), and the clarity of its surface. Also make a note of the position of the

moon at that specific time, i.e. from horizon to horizon, imagine a scale of 100 when in the centre of the sky, the setting will be 50, etc.

Set aside four minutes a day to record the weather. Study the four directions (north, east, south and west) and make notes of the amount of clouds and their appearance, i.e. fluffy, streaky, thick, heavy etc. The ideal times will be early morning, noon, late afternoon and early evening. Rain normally approaches from the same direction and moves away in similar fashion.

After the whole period, combine the information and notice the patterns that forecast rain. You can now prepare for a rain ceremony when the signs are clear.

6

DIVINATION TOOLS

It sounds rather strange to refer to a Sangoma's divination tools as a set of bones as they contain only a few actual bones. Some refer to them as 'dice' which is also misleading as they may not contain an actual die itself. Basically they consist of items such as bones, stones, shells, tablets etc. that hold symbolic value for the Sangoma herself. These bones are very personal and are probably the most valuable items she will ever possess. They are irreplaceable and she guards them with her life.

As with most traditional belief systems, the different tribes have their own unique way of divining, of which the bones are no exception. Probably the simplest set of bones is to be found among the Venda tribe and it is therefore appropriate to start with these.

In order to allow the reader to experience the information and to follow the divining process at first hand, I have tried to link this to the Western ways of divining. Chapter 7 is totally dedicated to finding the Western equivalents while Chapter 8 is all about how to interpret these. The similarities are astounding – it is almost as if both the African and Western processes were taught by the same teacher but in two different languages.

VENDA DIVINATION TABLETS

There are only four bones in this set. They are usually constructed from the tusks of an elephant or a wild boar and are roughly triangular in shape with symbols engraved on one side. They symbolise a young

woman, an old woman, a young man and an old man. They produce up to sixteen different possibilities when cast as dice and a further sixty-five when the top and bottom variants are taken into account. For the purpose of this book, we will study only the first sixteen variations.

In more detail, the tablets represent the following:

- **Young woman**   Like a breath of fresh air, the young woman is the daughter that stirs the family. She brings creativity and represents the mind and thinking.
- **Young man**   Bursting with energy and with fire in his veins, the young man is the son that brings vibrancy into the family. He represents blood and intuition.
- **Old woman**   This mature woman is the caring, yet practical mother that provides a nurturing environment. She represents reproduction, motherhood and the five senses.
- **Old man**   The mature man is the strong life-giving father on whom we depend for our keep, like the soil depends on water. He represents semen, rain, the power of life and feelings.

CASTING THE TABLETS

The tablets are cast by hand on to the ground as if they were dice. As mentioned before, sixteen combinations are possible. The tablets that fall face down are considered to be inactive (silent) while those with their symbols visible are actively involved (they speak). The sixteen different possibilities with their faces up are as follows:

- **Daughter**   Artistic talent, innocence, naivety (danger), spirituality, beauty, new blood into family.
- **Son**   Over-reacting, slow down, too fast, lava (danger), intuition, restraint, possible health problem.
- **Mother**   Fury of protective mother, nurturing, motherhood, home life, caring, practical matters, five senses.
- **Father**   Richness or total failure, power of life, stubbornness, rain, emotions, feelings.
- **Father and mother**   Good combination, good decisions, good advice, good crops, two mature forces assisting each other.

- **Father and daughter**   Daughter draws riches from father, bringing forth new love, new ideas, new life and new friendships.
- **Father and son**   Excess masculine energy, caution is called for, do not overdo, patience is needed, slow but steady progress.
- **Father, mother and daughter**   Daughter manipulates father, creating a dangerous situation that may result in an ending, loss or an illness.
- **Father, mother and son**   A dangerous situation, postpone plans, fear, something has been overlooked, the son stirs the mature forces with his energy.
- **Father, mother, daughter and son**   Best combination possible, harmony, love and knowledge, time is right, the answer is yes.
- **Father, son and daughter**   A silent situation, listen to your inner voice, hear your ancestors, use your inner guidance.
- **Mother and daughter**   Excess feminine energy, time to rest, nothing is happening, slow period, not good and not bad.
- **Mother and son**   Son's energy and Mother's nurturing, fertility, travel, further studies, plan properly, take care.
- **Mother, daughter and son**   Dishonesty (danger), weakness, things could get out of hand, use caution.
- **Son and daughter**   Energy, good combination that can overcome difficulties, plan properly, do not rush things.
- **All blank sides up**   Postpone all plans, investigate intentions, very low energy, time to regain strength, most negative combination.

A Sangoma 'hears and sees' through the ancestors while the bones 'speak' by the way they have fallen. The divination bones used by the other tribes discussed in this book are all very similar. The description that follows is closest to the Zulu tribe and may vary slightly from the other tribes.

Other Divination Bones

The four tablets found in the Venda set of bones are at the core of most other divination bones, although actual bones instead of tusks

are used by most other tribes. These symbolise the direct family of the patient. The bone of a male animal is used to represent the male energies, and a female animal's bone for the female energies.

Found in a set of bones are objects that represent all the main aspects of a person's life. Every aspect will have a small and a larger object that represent the female and the male respectively with one side as positive and the other negative. The way in which these objects fall reveals much about the interaction between the people and their environment.

Symbolic representations of the following are generally included in a set of bones:

- family of the patient, mother, father, son and daughter
- other people in the village, neighbours, and kin
- health, healing, medicine, medicine man
- the village
- the chief, advice, guidance
- the ancestors, male and female
- the enemy, witches, sorcerers
- courage, virility, weaponry
- brideswealth, household appliances
- immortality, death, loss
- secrets, unknown factors
- kindness, help offered
- wealth, crops, cattle
- luck, good and bad
- time, present and future.

The articles used are all chosen for their symbolic association. Traditionally the following items were used, although it is not always possible to find these today:

- bones of almost any animal – hyena, snake, dog, lion, antelope
- leopard bones, teeth, nails
- tortoise shell and bones
- stones – different shapes and sizes
- shells – abalone, sea, nut, urchins
- dice and dominoes.

Next I shall explore in a more detailed manner, the individual objects in a set of bones.

- **Immediate family**   Normally the bones from the ankle of a sheep are used for the immediate family of the patient. A large and small bone from both a male and a female sheep will represent the four human energies previously discussed under the Venda tablets. When the querant is, for example, a young woman, then the bone representing the daughter would be herself while the others would symbolise her immediate family.
  The bone from an ankle joint has a hollow part on the one side and a cupped part on the other, representing the positive and negative sides to each of these personalities. The open side is considered negative (imagine an open hand with greedy intent) while the closed side is positive (imagine a fist for protection).
- **People in the village**   The bones of goats are used to symbolise other people in the village and once again, the same rule applies, i.e. bones from a male animal for the male energies, and so on. These also have distinct differences on either side of each bone, one positive and the other negative.
- **Health**   Health is an important aspect in everyone's life and two bones from a bone-eating bushpig are normally used to symbolise this. The larger will be a medicine man, the smaller a medicine woman. The positive side up will indicate recovery and the negative side up will mean further suffering.
- **The village**   The bones from a territorial animal, such as a baboon, are used to show the village itself, as this is also territorial. The village in more modern times will represent the home environment of a person.
- **The chief**   A bone from a lion is used to indicate the chief. In this particular case only one bone is used as there is only one chief. The positive and the negative will be determined by which side of the bone is face up.
- **The ancestors**   Nocturnal animals that live underground carry the symbolic value of the ancestors. Two bones, one smaller than the other, will determine whether a male or female ancestor is involved in the current affairs of the patient. The positive side up will indicate approval while the negative side up shows displeasure.

- **Witches and sorcerers**   The bones from a hyena are appropriately marked as the symbol of witches and sorcerers. Once again a small and a large bone will indicate the female and male aspects while the positive and the negative will determine whether or not they are actively involved in the situation.
- **Courage and virility**   Two oliva shells are used to symbolise courage, virility and fighting spirit in young men. Both the small and the large shells refer to male energy. The small shell would be interpreted as hostility while the large shell would indicate courage. The closed side will count as the positive while the open side is negative results.
- **Brideswealth**   Two cowrie shells are used for female attributes such as brideswealth and birth. Again the large shell would indicate a good energy while the smaller shell would indicate a lazy attitude. The open side up will indicate a negative and the closed side up a positive result.
- **Immortality**   This is sometimes symbolised by tiger's eye stones which are often referred to as crocodile stones. It is said that these stones are found in the stomach of a crocodile but this is probably due to the similarity between the stones and the eyes of the animal. Many people lose their lives to crocodiles and it is therefore appropriate to make this association.
  Again two sizes are required. The smaller is seen as the negative energy while the larger stone symbolises the positive energy. One side will show positive, the other negative.
- **Secrets**   Turtle or tortoise shells or bones are connected to secrecy as the turtle hides from the outside world. In modern times two keys can symbolise the same thing, meaning the locking away of the secrets. The larger key would symbolise good secrets while the smaller key indicates bad secrets. The key must have a groove that runs along the straight part and when falling face up, it would be considered as open, i.e. secret is revealed. The closed side up (falling with the groove down) indicates that the secret is kept.
- **Kindness**   Assistance from neighbours and kin is often needed and these attributes are associated with the bones of a springbok or the shell from a nut. Once again two different sizes indicate

two different intents behind the kindness with positive as active and negative as inactive.

- **Wealth, crops and cattle**   Wealth, measured by successful crops and numerous cattle, is traditionally symbolised by cattle bones and teeth or leopard bones and teeth. More appropriately for modern times, two coins will suffice. One coin a little smaller than the other, indicating either good or bad wealth, while one side (heads) is positive and the other (tails) negative.
- **Luck**   Luck is as much a part of life in Africa as it is anywhere else in the world and an object that symbolises this is, traditionally, an abalone shell. Two dice of different sizes could be used in a modern set of bones. The same rule applies – the larger indicating good luck and the smaller bad luck. When using dice, the number indicated can then be interpreted even further.
- **Knowledge**   Knowledge was traditionally supplied by the chief as the ruler and therefore lion bones were often used to symbolise this aspect of leadership. As indicated above, under the heading 'Chief', wise knowledge and good guidance would be shown with the positive side of the bone falling face up, while the opposite would warn of wrong advice leading to bad guidance.
- **Time**   The Sangoma from a village far from the sea probably had no shells to use in her set to symbolise time. Two spiral shells are normally used with the larger one showing the future and the smaller one the more immediate timespan. The further an object falls from the small shell, the further into the future it can be expected to occur.

A stick, about 30 cm (12 inches) long could also be used to calculate time with each measure equivalent to one month. The whole stick would therefore indicate a year. This was used to calculate how far away a certain happening was from the client, by measuring the distance between two specific objects.

All of the above mentioned articles are collected over the period of training and initiation. Each holds value for the Sangoma in that she shares an experience with every one of them and they become part of her life. They are all selected with great care and become the link between her and the lessons she has learned during her initiation.

OTHER NECESSARY TOOLS

A number of other items are still required to complete the Sangoma's set of divination bones:

- **Snuff** A little container of snuff will always be found with the Sangoma's bones. This is normally taken prior to a consultation and after a couple of hearty sneezes, her head is clear enough to allow the ancestors to communicate through her. Snuff is also sprinkled around and over the bones to prevent any bad energy from interfering with the consultation.

- **Cow's tail** A cow's tail is necessary if and when the Sangoma throws the bones on to the bare ground. She would sweep the area first, removing all the little stones and sticks that may interfere in the way the bones must fall. It is also a way of chasing away the bad energies that may wish to manipulate the outcome of the fall.

- **Drum** Some Sangomas will carry with them a small drum, made of wood and animal skin, to awaken the ancestors from their sleep. This becomes more effective when more than one person takes part by clapping their hands to the rhythm of the drum. A dance may accompany this ritual during which the diviner will go into a trance.

- **Clothing** There are a number of items worn by a Sangoma that set her aside from ordinary folk, normally passed on to her by her teacher. Amongst these is her head covering – consisting generally of artificial hair with beads at the end. She will always wear at least two strings of beads that cross over her chest.

- **Divination mat** Normally the bones are cast on to a mat, made of grass, which sets the limits of the reading. The articles that fall on top of the mat form part of the consultation while those that fall off the mat are not involved at all. They remain where they have fallen and are picked up only when the reading is over.

Traditional Sangoma

The procedure

All Sangoma bone readings are done on the floor or on the ground. When an area outside is used, it will first be swept clean, after which the mat is placed in position. The area around the mat is

A Sangoma casting her 'bones'

sprinkled with snuff and at this stage the diviner may sniff some herself, resulting in a few head-clearing sneezes.

The Sangoma takes the complete set of bones into her two cupped hands, while her breathing becomes sharp and jerky (almost like hiccups). She allows her outbreath to flow over the bones (some ask the patient to do the same) and after a while she casts the bones on to the mat. After a period of carefully studying the fall, she starts her interpretation.

EXERCISE 7
ASSOCIATIONS

Using Chapter 5 as a guideline, you can at this stage make a list of areas of importance that you wish to have represented in a set of 'bones'. By doing this, you can produce a set designed to cater for your unique needs.

One way to go about this is, first, to take an ordinary day and take note of the different situations and people actively involved in that day. Then take a special day such as a birthday and take note of the same situations and people. Continue doing this until all possibilities have been covered.

Another way would be to look at the immediate area that you occupy, i.e. the space on which you stand or sit. Take note of your needs here and now and then let the picture grow. Be aware of how your needs grow at the same tempo that your environment expands and continue doing this until you have included the whole universe.

Now make your list and find objects that carry symbolic value for you and connect these two lists. The only limit placed upon the number of objects is the size of your hands when held cupped together. You need to make sure that you can actually cast these with ease.

7 WESTERN SIMILARITIES

When an unfamiliar topic is studied, all the information that is absorbed is stored in the brain until an association is made. A common expression for this is when 'the penny drops' – then it is understood.

The purpose of this chapter is to allow the penny to drop by connecting the information from Chapter 6 with better-known Western topics to enable you to identify with old knowledge and thereby understand this complex African system.

ELEMENT TABLETS

There are many Western equivalents of the four tablets used by the Venda tribe. The first is the four court cards in the Tarot and they are, in a nutshell, four personalities: two male and two female of which two are mature and two are immature. They connect to the tablets as follows:

Tablets	Family	Tarot	Personalities
Old man	Father	King	Mature man
Old woman	Mother	Queen	Mature woman
Young man	Son	Knight	Immature man
Young woman	Daughter	Page	Immature woman

The most striking coincidental association is found in the four symbols of the *Tetregrammaton*, one of the seventy-two names of God found in the Torah. Yehovah is considered the Holy name of God and is pronounced as *YUD-HE-VAV-HE* (YHVH), referring to the four Hebrew letters that make up the name.

The four suits of the Tarot and the letters are linked to the same energies as mentioned above and, although not in the same sequence, are as follows:

Hebrew	Family	Tarot	Element	Suit	Symbol
Yud	Father	King	Fire	Wands	△
He	Mother	Queen	Water	Cups	▽
Vav	Son	Knight	Air	Swords	△
He	Daughter	Page	Earth	Pentacles	▽

By using the four elements as the main focus, you can now produce a set of tablets. A few suggestions follow:

- Use a natural material such as wood or clay and make four rectangular-shaped tablets. A good size would be roughly 30 mm long × 20 mm wide × 5 mm thick. Once you are 100 per cent fluent with the sixteen variations, triangular tablets can be made and the other possibilities studied.
- Use symbols that connect to the elements and paint or carve these on to the tablet. It would probably be easier to start by writing or painting the name of the element on to the tablet, i.e. Water, Air, Fire, and Earth. A few symbolic suggestions are:

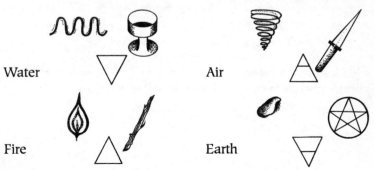

Water   Air

Fire   Earth

- When casting the tablets, use the hand opposite to writing, i.e. the left hand for a right-handed person and vice versa. This way a good connection will be made with the subconscious and the tablets are more likely to show the subtle underlying issues at play.

Although the meaning of the tablets and the way they fall will remain very much the same as set out in the previous chapter, what follows is a more Western approach to the interpretation:

1 **Fire** on its own can be dangerous, although the odds of a disaster increase when some of the other elements are present.
2 **plus Water** combined can produce steam if handled with care, or the Water can extinguish the Fire when used carelessly. Therefore, a good energy can be expected but it should be handled with patience.
3 **plus Air** Air fuels the Fire which can then easily get out of hand, so once again caution and patience are needed. When the planning is done properly, the energy is present and achievement is within reach.
4 **plus Earth** Soil is fertilised when grass is burned by Fire and this combination has major potential yet to be explored. Further work is required to reach the goals and an investigation is called for.
5 **Water** on its own cannot be contained and it is therefore either richness or poverty. Its potential depends on the presence of the other elements.
6 **plus Air** Water contained in Air is nothing more than a cloud that produces rain, indicating new growth. A new romance, friendship or a new idea is on its way.
7 **plus Earth** When Earth contains Water, a lake or river is produced that can carry the nourishment to where it is needed or store it until the need is present. A good combination that will bring forth equally good results.
8 **Air** as a single element can often be misjudged as it is not visible. A strong wind will cause disruption, while a cool breeze will bring relief on a hot day. Stale Air on the other hand is stifling and suffocating.

9 **plus Earth**   This combination produces deserts and therefore calls for silence. No growth, nor the potential thereof is present and a third element is necessary to change this status quo.

10 **Earth**   on its own may hold the seeds but without the other elements, cannot promote growth. It therefore warns of danger connected to the seeds held within. It is a nurturing energy that is waiting to produce all its potential.

11 **Fire, Water, Air and Earth**   together create completion and total harmony resulting in the best possibilities. This energy will bring love, knowledge and achievement.

12 **Fire, Water and Air**   cannot manifest and inner guidance is therefore called for when this combination is the result of a throw. The Earth's nurturing qualities are missing and help will come from the higher mind.

13 **Water, Air and Earth**   together create a situation that lacks the energy provided by Fire and therefore shows a weakness somewhere, calling for caution. A storm is brewing that may cause the ending of a relationship. Lightning is likely to strike and therefore an illness is possible.

14 **Fire, Air and Earth**   together form a dangerous situation that warns of dishonesty aimed against the querant. The situation is without Water (emotion) and therefore unbalanced.

15 **Fire, Water and Earth**   is another situation that calls for caution as something has been overlooked. Water and Fire produce steam and when Earth is added, a flood may be the result.

16 **All the tablets fall face down**
This is the worst possible combination and calls for all plans to be postponed as a void is created. These tablets are effective and not only do they answer questions, they also offer advice and guidance. As an example let us look at the combination (number **15** above) of Fire, Water and Earth together. As explained earlier, this combination warns of something that has been overlooked. Once Air is added to this combination, the probability of success increases greatly. One can then advise the querant to be a little more logical (Air = thinking) and re-evaluate the situation.

To follow is a table of further links to the four elements:

Element	Suit	Function	Level	Season
Fire	Wands	Intuition	Spirit	Summer
Water	Cups	Emotion	Soul	Spring
Air	Swords	Logic	Ego	Autumn
Earth	Pentacles	Sensory	Body	Winter

Sangoma bones

The African Sangoma bones can easily be modified to suit the Western reader and to follow is a selection of items that, if and when readily available in the environment, can be collected to symbolise the different aspects of day-to-day life. These items are merely suggestions and should an object reflect an aspect of a different kind, then you should change this to suit yourself. This is, after all, a personal way of divining and the whole system will change accordingly.

1 **Immediate family**   As mentioned before, normally the bones from the ankle joint of a sheep will be used to symbolise the immediate family of the querant. Next time a leg of lamb is purchased, ask the butcher to include the ankle joint. This part should then be boiled until the bones are separated from the flesh. Soak these in a solution containing bleach and soon a selection of small, clean bones will be available. The hollow section indicates negative, the 'closed' side is positive and when on its side, movement is taking place, i.e. the person is moving away from something.

Another option is to use the four Element tablets instead of bones. The interpretations as set out above can then be incorporated with the other items still to be discussed.

People in the village – other people This aspect can be changed to symbolise other people, such as colleagues, neighbours, friends, etc. but is not essential. There are many possibilities for the use of the Divination Mat and it is therefore recommended to leave this aspect out of the modified version. The reason for this will become clearer at the end of this chapter.

2 **Health** Health is an important aspect of the lives of most people and appropriate symbolic items to use here are two tiger's eye stones. Although they represent Immortality in the Sangoma's set of bones, they could serve well as health indicators in the modified selection of bones.

Two sizes are required with one side of each stone marked as positive and the other negative. Spend a little time with these stones and 'feel' which side is more positive than the other. The marking can easily be achieved by painting + and – with nail varnish on to the stones. The larger of the two will show good health while the smaller will show bad health. The positive side up will indicate recovery while the negative side up will warn of further suffering.

3 **The village – home** As mentioned before, the village will represent the home environment of a person. Two open shells have been chosen for these connections since these are the 'homes' of the sea animal. The larger will be the positive while the smaller will show the negative. The open side shows an open house while the closed end is the opposite.

4 The chief – teacher Although guidance comes in many forms, this particular aspect is from another living person and two teeth have been selected, as guidance comes through words spoken by mouth. One can obtain sheep or cattle teeth from a butcher, one small and one big. The big tooth will indicate good guidance while the small one will indicate bad guidance. The front part of the tooth will be positive (advice taken) and the back part negative (advice ignored).

5 The ancestors – spiritual guides The presence of spiritual guides is probably more acceptable to the Western reader than that of ancestors, even though they may well be the same thing. To symbolise these, a long bone is cut in two with one side a little shorter than the other. This bone can be obtained from the same leg of lamb used earlier and cleaned in the same way.
A 'broken' bone shows a broken life, indicating a spiritual being. The guidance itself may be the same as that offered by the two teeth, but in this particular case it will be from the spirit. The larger bone will show a male guide and the smaller a female. The positive side up (open side or positively marked) will indicate pleasure while the negative side will show displeasure.

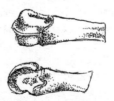

6 Witches and sorcerers – manipulation Manipulation is as much a part of life in the West as it is in Africa and the symbol of this is the pine cone, indicating an unplanted seed, i.e. wasted potential. Once again there is a small cone and a large cone with a positive and a negative side, giving four possibilities. 'Good' manipulation with good or bad intent and 'bad' manipulation with good or bad intent.

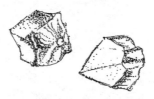

7 **Courage and virility – masculine**   Two oliva shells are used to symbolise courage, virility and fighting spirit in young men in a set of Sangoma bones. In the modified version, the same qualities are symbolised, although these are not necessarily only in male persons. Every human being, both male and female, has masculine and feminine qualities in their make-up. The masculine aspects are represented here and include assertiveness and courage, both positive and negative, with good and bad results.

8 **Bridewealth – feminine**   The cowrie shells in the Sangoma's bones are used for the female attributes such as love, caring and feeling. Again the large shell would indicate a good energy while the small shell will show a bad attribute. The open side up will indicate a negative and the closed side up a positive result to these energies.
The round side of these shells causes them to roll over and fall with their open side down, resulting in the negative side mainly down. In order to get a fair possibility, the reader can level this

end by using sand paper in order to create a flat surface. Even though it breaks open the shell, it would still be read as closed side down.

9 **Immortality – reincarnation** A piece of wood is used to symbolise this aspect as, even though the tree may not be alive, the wood continues to live in the form of furniture or fire. Only one piece is used with a positive point on the one side and a negative point on the other. To mark these, the bark can be removed and a positive and negative marking made with a pen. One should keep in mind the wheel of reincarnation and the role that past and future lives play in the present. This aspect would cover karmic debts brought into this life and new debts being created in the present.

10 **Secrets** Two keys are all that is needed to show this aspect. The larger will show a positive and the smaller a negative secret. The open end (with the groove up) will indicate that the secret is revealed while the closed end (with the groove down) will show a kept secret.

11 **Kindness – assistance**   Kindness or assistance is appreciated by all human beings and this area is symbolised by two rose quartz stones, symbolising an offering. Once again two different sizes indicate two different intents behind the kindness, with positive as active and negative as inactive. Use your intuitive powers to determine the positive (good) and negative (bad) sides of each stone.

12 **Wealth, crops and cattle – money matters**   Wealth, measured in monetary value is symbolised by two coins, one a little smaller than the other, indicating large and small amounts. The positive side (financial gain) is shown when heads is face up while the negative (financial loss) is indicated when tails is face up.

13 **Luck**   Luck is as much a part of life in Africa as it is anywhere else in the world and a single die symbolises this aspect. The number that falls face up will indicate the possibilities. The number 5 will show a change in luck while even numbers (2, 4, 6 and 8) will indicate bad luck. Uneven numbers (1, 3, 7 and 9) are interpreted as good luck.

Knowledge – teacher   Knowledge is passed on by the teacher and can therefore be seen as guidance, as discussed previously.

14   Time   The two spiral shells used by a Sangoma can be used with the larger shell the distant future (approximately 12 months) and the smaller shell showing the immediate future. The further an object falls from the small shell, the further into the future it can be expected to occur. Positive and negative possibilities will be indicated by the fall of the other objects in the reading.

Summary

The above information may, at this stage, seem too much to absorb but, when seen in totality, it becomes much easier to understand. Please take note that the author uses keywords for lack of space only and you can expand considerably within these guidelines.

To follow is a summary of a modern set of bones as set out previously and accompanied by their meanings. They have been numbered individually in order to assist you with the interpretation in Chapter 8.

1a	Family	Father	+	Good provider, supportive, emotional
			–	Stubborn, hard, selfish, stingy, moody
1b		Mother	+	Nurturing, caring, giving, practical
			–	Self-centred, shrewd, critical, dull
1c		Son	+	Energetic, intuitive, fun loving
			–	Promiscuous, nasty, arrogant, impatient
1d		Daughter	+	Intelligent, artistic, dreamer, friendly
			–	Sarcastic, nasty, critical, aggressive

2a	Health	Large	+	Good health continues
			–	Health at risk, take care, rest plenty
2b		Small	+	Recovering from bad health
			–	Bad health persists, beware of accident
3a	Home	Large	+	Friendly, nurturing home open
			–	Friendly, nurturing home closed
3b		Small	+	Unfriendly home open
			–	Unfriendly home closed
4a	Teacher	Large	+	Good advice given and taken
			–	Good advice given, but not taken
4b		Small	+	Bad advice given and taken
			–	Bad advice given, but not taken
5a	Spiritual guides	Large	+	Male guide expressing pleasure
			–	Male guide expressing concern
5b		Small	+	Female guide expressing pleasure
			–	Female guide expressing concern
6a	Manipu- lation	Large	+	Good intent with good result
			–	Good intent with bad result
6b		Small	+	Bad intent with good result
			–	Bad intent with bad result
7a	Masculine	Large	+	Assertive skills with good result
			–	Assertive skills with bad result
7b		Small	+	Aggression with good result
			–	Aggression with bad result
8a	Feminine	Large	+	Affection with good intent and good result
			–	Affection with good intent and bad result
8b		Small	+	Affection with bad intent and good result
			–	Affection with bad intent and bad result
9	Reincarnation		+	Good karma created
			–	Bad karma created
10a	Secrets	Large	+	Good secret revealed
			–	Good secret remains hidden
10b		Small	+	Bad secret revealed
			–	Bad secret remains hidden
11a	Assistance	Large	+	Kind assistance offered and accepted
			–	Kind assistance withheld
11b		Small	+	Negative help offered and accepted
			–	Negative help withheld

12a Money matters	Large	H	Large financial gain
		T	Large financial loss
12b	Small	H	Small financial gain
		T	Small financial loss
13 Luck	Odd		Good luck connected with 1, 3, 7, or 9
	Even		Bad luck connected with 2, 4, 6, or 8
	5		Luck is in the process of changing
14a Time	Present		At the present moment
14b	Future		Within the next few months – from 1 to 12 max

Once you are familiar with the meanings of the various objects, the positions in which they fall becomes important. When two objects touch each other, a significant meaning will be attached to this; for instance, if a bone should fall on top of a coin, then the person represented by the bone is involved in finances. Whether it is good or bad will depend on whether the positive or the negative side of both the bone and the coin is face up.

The different possibilities are discussed in Chapter 8 where six variations are studied in detail.

Divination Mat

An even deeper meaning can be attached when one uses a traditional Divination Mat, sometimes used by the Zulu Sangoma. The design of the mat and the twelve houses of the Astrological Natal Chart are amazingly similar, although one does not interpret them in the same manner.

The qualities included in the table below have been connected to astrology merely to assist the Western student in associating this with a better researched topic.

It is easy to construct and can be used either with or without the bones symbolising the family included in the set. Use the following guidelines to construct your own Divination mat:

1   Use a piece of leather, cloth or any other natural material. The design can also be drawn on to a firm area of soil. It may be advisable to start with a piece of paper.

2   Draw a circle with a diameter of approximately 30 cm (12 inches), or a radius of 15 cm (6 inches) on the above.

3   Divide the circle into twelve segments, i.e. 30° angles, similar to a round cake that is divided into twelve portions. First divide the circle of 360° into four quarters (each 90°), then subdivide each quarter into three (each 30°) parts.

4   The four energies that were earlier connected to the four elements are now repeated three times. To follow is a reminder of the good and bad attributes present in the four elements.

- Fire   Energy, youthful, arrogant, enthusiastic, impatient, intuitive

- Earth   Practical, capable, dull, shrewd, obstinate, lazy, nurturing.

- Air   Intelligent, friendly, sarcastic, communicative, artistic.

- Water   Intuitive, emotional, sympathetic, moody, kind.

5   As mentioned before the qualities used by the author are those used in astrology and they are briefly as follows:

- Cardinal Decision-maker, courageous, will-power, will get own way, initiator.

- Fixed   Loyal, inflexible, stubborn, hate to give in, will stick with situation.

- Mutable   Flexible, versatile, lack perseverance, cope with change.

When the above qualities and energies are combined, twelve variants are created. As an example, let us look at the fire element combined with the four qualities. Cardinal Fire will be similar to the initial burst of the flame when a match is struck while Fixed Fire is similar to the end piece of the wood burning. Mutable Fire can be compared with the glow (promise of Fire) in the match after it is spent. Similarly, all the other Elements will have three variants as set out below.

The author has used the same design as an astrological natal chart and inserted the sun signs in the table below. See the Divination Mat diagram later in this chapter.

No	Degrees	Element	Person	Energy	Quality	Sun sign
1	270–240	Fire	Son	Young man	Cardinal	Aries
2	240–210	Earth	Mother	Mature woman	Fixed	Taurus
3	210–180	Air	Daughter	Young woman	Mutable	Gemini
4	180–150	Water	Father	Mature man	Cardinal	Cancer
5	150–120	Fire	Son	Young man	Fixed	Leo
6	120–90	Earth	Mother	Mature woman	Mutable	Virgo
7	90–60	Air	Daughter	Young woman	Cardinal	Libra
8	60–30	Water	Father	Mature man	Fixed	Scorpio
9	30–360	Fire	Son	Young man	Mutable	Sagittarius
10	360–330	Earth	Mother	Mature woman	Cardinal	Capricorn
11	330–300	Air	Daughter	Young woman	Fixed	Aquarius
12	300–270	Water	Father	Mature man	Mutable	Pisces

When the Divination Mat is used, one would determine first the sun sign of the querant. All the objects that fall within that particular segment will reflect directly on him or her. Other segments will reflect on other people born under different sun signs. The use of the bones and/or tablets is not necessary when the mat is used.

EXERCISE 8
COLLECTING OWN SET

Using the information gathered during the previous exercise and in this chapter, you are now ready to collect your own associated objects. Spend time with each object and connect to the energy held within. The better you know them the better they will serve you. Enjoy!

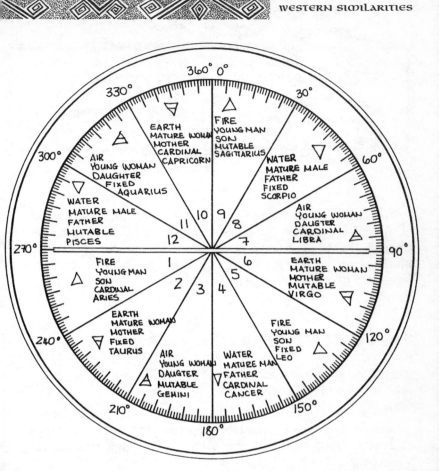

Divination Mat

8

SAMPLE
READINGS

The following six readings were created by the artist and left to the author to interpret. The number system used in the summary in Chapter 7 is used to help you distinguish between the various objects. All the pieces in these readings are marked and the connecting lines have been drawn to assist you.

INTERPRETATION

In order to make sure that all aspects of the bones are taken into account, use the following steps:

1 Determine who the querant is, i.e. mature man [1a], mature woman [1b], young man [1c], or young woman [1d] and then look at things from that perspective, i.e. positive, negative or moving.
2 Take note of all the articles that have fallen off the mat – these aspects are not involved in the reading.
3 Notice which pieces are on top of one another or touch each other. These are significant situations as they interlink.
4 Draw imaginary lines between the querant and the other people and take note of what lies between these. They will indicate possible problems between these two people.
5 Use the time pieces to determine the timespan of the particular spread by measuring the distance between the two pieces. Approximately 1 inch would indicate 1 month with the maximum

of 12 months. When and if one piece is off the mat, the time is unknown and should be stated as such.

6　When two of the same objects fall together with opposite faces up, it indicates that things are in the process of changing.

7　Use the mat to signify the querant on the sun sign, i.e. the objects that fall within that space are connected with querant.

READING ONE

Querant:　Mature male feeling negative (possibly worried) [1a–].

Off mat:　[4b], [9], [11a], [11b] and [13] – No assistance, no luck and no karma involved in situation.

Time:　Path D – Approximately 1 month (1 inch). [1a–] on path – Mature male will be affected most by situation.

Touching:　[1a–], [14b], [6a+] – Although querant is stubborn at the moment, he will manipulate the situation with good intent and good results within the next month.
[1a–], [12aH], [8b–], [5b–] – Querant stands to gain a large amount of money by demonstrating false affection, causing displeasure from a female spirit in the next month.
[5a+], [14a] – Male guide is expressing pleasure at the current situation.
[3a+], [3b–], [1c–] – Young arrogant male person from an unfriendly home, changing it to a friendlier environment.
[1d side], [10a–], [8a+] – Young female uninvolved and unable to express affection due to an unrevealed secret.
[7b+], [4a–] – Aggressive advice is given but not taken.
[1b side], [2b–] – Mature female uninvolved due to illness or recent death.

Connect:　Path A – [6b+] and [3b–] on path – Mature male may need to use bad manipulation in order to win situation in unfriendly home and should use caution as small financial loss may occur [12bT].
Path B – [8b–] – on path – Young woman feels rejected by mature male.
Path C – Clear.

Summary: It appears that the mother in this family has recently died, or is in the process of dying, and the father wants the son to live with him. Both males are negative while both females appear to be uninvolved. The daughter knows something that the father is not aware of and she chooses to remain silent. The father is probably hoping to inherit money while the daughter knows different. It appears that only through manipulation will this situation work itself out as no help is offered and luck is not involved. It will take one month for all this to come to pass.

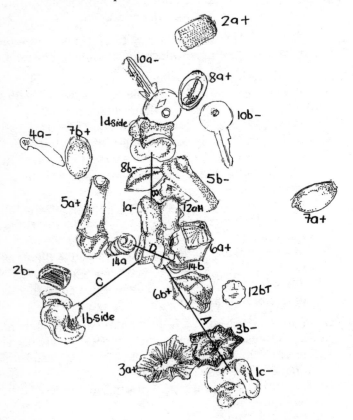

Reading one

READING TWO

Querant: Young woman [1d] – not in fall, i.e. not active in reading.

Off mat: [1d], [4a], [7b], [9], [11a], [11b], [13].

Time: Path D – Approximately 2 months (2 inches). [7a+] on path touching [14a] – Assertive skills with good results active at present.

Touching: [12aH], [3a–], [3b–], [6b+] – A large sum of money is hidden in one of two closed homes. Access is barred. [2b–], [1a–], [10b–] – A mature male person is very ill and is keeping it well hidden. Recovery is possible if he follows advice given and seeks help [4b+], [10a+], [2a+]. [1b+], [14b] – Mature female may be able to offer her affection within the next 2 months.

Connect: Path A – [2b–] on path – The illness is stopping these two mature people from connecting.
Path B – [2b–] and [5b+] on path – Female guide is preventing young male from realising what the problem is.
Path C – Clear

Summary: The querant may live away form parents, explaining why she is not actively involved. Both parents are aware of the money (nothing lies between these) but cannot access it – possibly invested. Father's illness may be hidden due to lack of money and it may be too late once this becomes available. The young man may be a brother or a lover who is too far removed from the situation to see things clearly. He tries with selfish intent [8b+], approved by a female guide [5b+] – probably indicating that the situation should not concern him. Help will not be offered by someone else and the best way out is for the father to seek medical help as recovery is possible at this stage. A male guide [5a–] is not pleased about the lies that are being told.

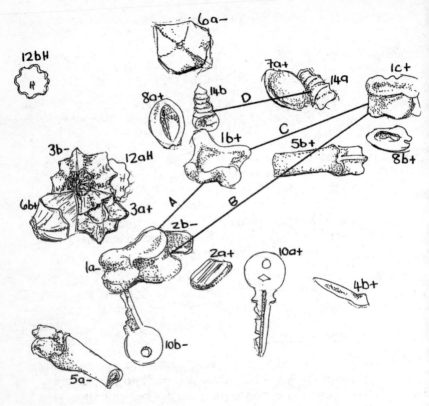

Reading two

READING THREE

Querant: Mature woman [1b side] – moving away from situation.

Off mat: [1c], [1d], [4a], [4b], [9], [11a], [11b], [12a].

Time: Path B – Approximately 3 months (~3 inches). [6b+] and [13.5] on path – Over the next 3 months manipulation will take place with good results as luck is changing.

Touching: [8a+], [10a–], [12bT], [6a+] – The knowledge of a small amount of money that has been lost is hidden to save someone from unnecessary hurt.

[7a+], [5b+] – Female guide is pleased with assertive skills demonstrated.

[1b side], [8b+] – Querant is turning her back on an unfriendly home and directing her affections elsewhere.

[10b–], [3b–], [3a+] – There is a bad secret connected to the unfriendly home but things are changing, although secret will not be revealed.

Connect: Path A – clear – Mature adults are both turning their backs on current situations.

Summary: Two mature people, male and female, are turning their backs on their situations and are possibly planning a future together. The woman is leaving behind an unhappy home that is undergoing changes although the secrets will not be revealed. The man is exercising his assertive skills, which pleases a female guide. He probably leaves behind an awkward financial situation form which he is currently protected by the same female guide. Bad manipulation, with fortunate good results will take place over the next three months that may save the man from changes in his health – [2a+] and [2b–] lie close to [1a]. Both these people have used their past – [6a+] lies between these two situations – to manipulate a better future for themselves. Luck may be on their side.

READING FOUR

Querant: Mature woman [1b–] – Probably worried about a child.

Off mat: [9], [10a], [11a], [11b], [13].

Time: Path A – Approximately 2 months (˜2 inches). [5a+] on path – Good male guidance will be available during next 2 months.

Touching: [1c+], [4a+], [5b+], [12aH], [10b–] – A young man has come into a large sum of money from an unknown

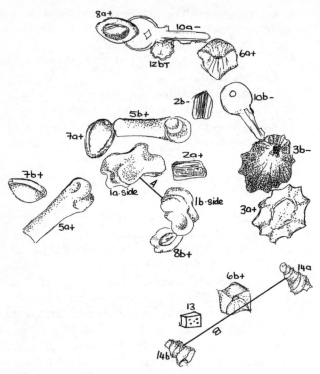

Reading three

source. He is given good advice which he pretends not to hear, causing pleasure from a female guide.

[2b–], [2a+], [12bH] – The young man's health is in the process of changing and it will require small financial assistance in the next two months, which will be forthcoming.

[5a+], [6b+], [6a–], [7a+], [3a–], [14a] – Good male guidance is assisting him to use his assertive skills (with good results) in order to escape a manipulative situations (that is busy changing) in an unfriendly home.

Connect: Path B and path E – [8a+] on both paths – Both parents are concerned about a young woman that is close to the young man.

Path C – clear – Two young people are close with nothing blocking them.

Summary: The querant and her husband are both concerned about their daughter who is involved with a young man from a shady background, although the husband is not as close to the daughter. The young man received a large amount of money recently, the source of which is unknown, and is currently making plans to move away. He will probably take the young lady with him, causing the parents distress. Future health problems will change the affection between these two people and the relationship will probably not survive these changes. The young lady will probably return to the friendly home she is leaving behind. The young man will turn aggressive towards his own family although at this stage things are still pleasant. There will be strong male guidance to assist him over the next two months.

READING FIVE

Querant: Mature woman [1b+] Happy and content.

Off mat: [2b], [4a], [5b], [7a], [11a], [11b], [13].

Time: Path A – Less than 1 month (less than 1 inch).

Touching: [12bH], [1b+] – Querant has acquired a small amount of money, making her feel secure and positive.
[3b–], [6a–], [10a–] – Manipulation in a closed, unfriendly home is being kept a secret.
[10b–], [1c side], [14b], [6b+], [3a+] – A young man is planning secretively to move away from an unfriendly home into an open friendly environment where he is likely to be manipulated by a negative young woman.

Connect: Path D – clear – Mature man is very distant – he probably lives apart from woman.
Path B – [6b+] on path – The young man is connected to the young woman by bad manipulation with good results. She probably makes good decisions on his behalf.
Path C – Clear

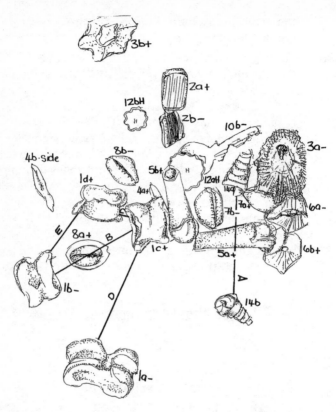

Reading four

Summary: The querant is unaware of the unhappiness experienced by her son at home. She feels secure with her financial situation while all affection, [8a+] and [8b+] is far removed from both her and her son. He on the other hand is planning secretly to move out within the next month, probably to join a girlfriend who at this stage is quite negative. The querant will realise this only once he has moved out. A male spiritual guide [5a+], who shared a past life with the querant [9] is at this stage pleased with the situation and is preventing her from becoming aggressive [7b+] in demonstrating her

affection [8b+]. Both these qualities will have good results if applied now, but the lesson has to be learned first. Her husband is not actively involved although he criticises her actions as he is negative.

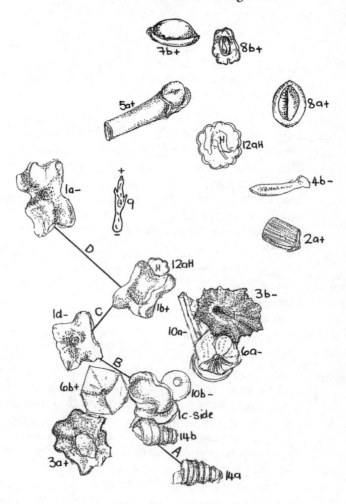

Reading five

READING SIX

Querant: Young female [1d–] – Currently negative.

Off mat: [1a], [2b], [4a], [4b], [9], [11b], [12b], [13].

Time: Path A – About 4 months (˜4 inches). [12aT], [10a–], [10b–] and [5a–] on path – Within 4 months a large amount of money will be lost. Displeased male guide is aware of the amount of money that is secretively being wasted.

Touching: [1d–], [7b+] – Querant is rightfully angry at the moment. [5b side], [10b–] – A bad secret is still unrevealed and kept this way by female guide assisting in the situation. [3a+], [14a], [5a–] – Friendly, open home is causing displeasure for male guide at the moment.
[8a+], [6b+], [11a–], [7a–] – Although there is great affection present, assistance from a kind source is deliberately held back while assertive skills are being used.

Connect: Path D – [1c–] on path – Young negative male person has come between two female persons.
Path B – clear – The mature woman understands the young man.
Path C – [7b+] on path – Querant's anger is towards young male that has come between her and mature woman.

Summary: Young woman is angry at a young man (either brother or lover) who probably told her mother about her extravagant lifestyle. The mother has in turn held back financial assistance although she cares about the querant. The mature woman is applying good manipulation [6a+] skills that will have good results by not bailing the daughter out at the moment. The young man on the other hand is jealous as the friendly open home is not open to him and the young woman's anger probably does not allow him to share her life. The whole situation will eventually (within 4 months) cost the mother quite a large amount and will have a taxing effect on the health of the young woman, although she will recover.

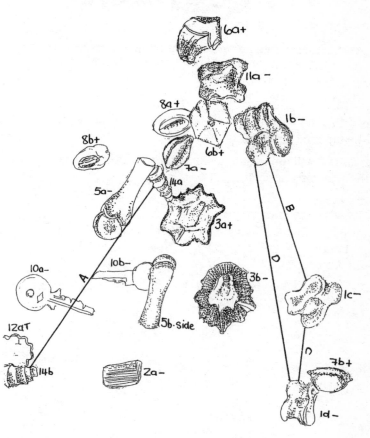

Reading six

feedback

The author hopes that you have enjoyed reading this book as much as she enjoyed writing it.

The author will appreciate feedback, both good and bad, in writing to the following address:

Kate Rheeders
P O Box 15239
Farrarmere
1518 Benoni
South Africa

OThER TITLES IN ThIS SERIES

Astral Projection 0 340 67418 0   £5.99
Becoming Prosperous 0 340 69773 3   £5.99
Chakras 0 340 62082 X   £5.99
Channelling 0 340 70472 1   £5.99
Chinese Horoscopes 0 340 64804 X   £5.99
Dowsing 0 340 60882 X   £5.99
Dream Interpretation 0 340 60150 7   £5.99
Earth Mysteries 0 340 70516 7   £5.99
Feng Shui 0 340 62079 X   £5.99
Gems and Crystals 0 340 60883 8   £5.99
The Goddess 0 340 68390 2   £5.99
Graphology 0 340 60625 8   £5.99
Herbs for Magic and Ritual 0 340 67415 6   £4.99
I Ching 0 340 62080 3   £5.99
Interpreting Signs and Symbols 0 340 68827 0   £5.99
Love Signs 0 340 64805 8   £5.99
The Magic and Mystery of Trees 0 340 70494 2   £5.99
Meditation 0 340 64835 X   £5.99
Mediumship 0 340 68009 1   £5.99
Numerology 0 340 59551 5   £5.99
Pagan Gods for Today's Man 0 340 69130 1   £5.99
Paganism 0 340 67013 4   £5.99
Palmistry 0 340 59552 3   £5.99
Qabalah 0 340 67339 7   £5.99
Reincarnation and You 0 340 70517 5   £5.99
Runes 0 340 62081 1   £5.99
Shamanism 0 340 68010 5   £5.99
Spiritual Healing 0 340 67416 4   £5.99
Star Signs 0 340 59553 1   £5.99
Tantric Sexuality 0 340 68349 X   £5.99
Tarot 0 340 59550 7   £5.99
The Moon and You 0 340 64836 8   £5.99
Visualisation 0 340 65495 3   £5.99
Witchcraft 0 340 67014 2   £5.99
Working With Colour 0 340 67011 8   £5.99
Your Psychic Powers 0 340 67417 2   £5.99